Praise for Li~~j~~
St. Thérèse of Lisieux

"Once again, Br. Joseph Schmidt leads us through the spiritual journey of experiencing the Divine in our daily lives. Using Thérèse's life experience and teachings as she listened to God, Br. Joe plumbs the depth of her transformation and awakening. His latest book stirs up the subtle, hidden, and powerful ways God is inviting us into intimacy and transformation in the very humanity of real life. His insights into this youngest Doctor of the Church enable us to see God in the ordinary of life where "everything is grace" and how to mentor our restless hearts in response to the restless and ever-present heart of God. This is a delightful, energizing, and easy read with profound and practical insights into how to live a life of grace and gratitude."
—Fr. Bob Colaresi, OCarm, Society of the Little Flower

"This is an extraordinary book written for the person seeking to live more peacefully and deepen his/her relationship with a loving God. The authors skillfully invite the reader to travel with Thérèse as there is a transformation from compulsive behavior to inner peace. She becomes an advocate for nonviolence for herself and toward others."
—Br. Bernard LoCoco, FSC, past president of Christian Brothers University, Memphis; former director of the SAT Sabbatical Program in Berkeley, California; and currently a spiritual director and teacher of spirituality

"Meet Thérèse of Lisieux 2.0, not your grandmother's 'Little Flower of Jesus.' The authors peel away the baggage and barnacles present in so many devotional biographies of Thérèse to reveal a clear-headed, focused, and self-aware young woman whose spiritual journey becomes familiar and accessible. Using Thérèse's own writings and a nuanced psycho-spiritual approach, the authors show how Thérèse comes to see, acknowledge, and name her 'addictions,' all the while resting and rejoicing in God's boundless love. Thérèse's Little Way is transformed from what many may have written off as a historical piety to a vibrant and doable spiritual practice. This young Doctor of the Church has something relevant to say to all of us!"
—Judith Ann Zielinski, OSF, Writer/ Producer/ Documentary filmmaker

"St. Thérèse of Lisieux is a wonderful companion for us as we seek a deeper intimacy with God and the realization of God's unconditional love for us. Marisa Guerin and Br. Joseph Schmidt have provided a new resource for a friendship with Thérèse in that search for God."
—Bishop Timothy Senior, Auxiliary Bishop of Philadelphia; rector, St. Charles Borromeo Seminary, Overbrook, Pennsylvania

"I consider my friend Br. Joe Schmidt, hands down, the world's expert on Thérèse and her Little Way of nonviolent love. Thanks to Marisa Guerin, Br. Joe was able to complete this last testament, and it's a masterpiece—just what we need!—Thérèse's life lessons put into understandable teachings for these turbulent times. Here we find the concrete steps of 'inner freedom, compassion, creativity, willingness, gratefulness and self-surrender' that can guide us to follow Jesus with confidence on the path of love and peace. Thérèse's conviction 'that God's love, justice, and mercy are utterly and always without violence,' forms the basis of her lessons and shows how we too, like Thérèse and Br. Joe, might break through our own personal struggles toward universal love, infinite compassion, and deeper peace, becoming Christ's instruments of peace and nonviolent love for our broken world."

—Fr. John Dear is the director of BeatitudesCenter.org and author of forty books, including *The Beatitudes of Peace* and *The God of Peace*. He was nominated for the Nobel Peace Prize by Archbishop Tutu.

"The life of St. Thérèse of Lisieux, the beloved 'Little Flower,' can seem so far removed from ours. Many of us think, 'Who could be as holy as she was?' But this beautiful new book draws practical and accessible lessons from her life and her writings, and is sure to be enormous help to anyone who wants to live a more meaningful, loving and peaceful life. It's like having St. Thérèse as your spiritual director."

—Fr. James Martin, SJ, author of *My Life with the Saints* and *Learning to Pray*

"Those familiar with the life of St Thérèse of Lisieux might wonder: could anything new possibly be discovered about her Little Way spirituality? Our two authors have decisively confirmed that delving deep into the Theresian seam still delivers unimaginable gems of wisdom. *Life Lessons* is a masterpiece by two aficionados: one, a De La Salle Brother who has devoted his ministry to making the Little Flower known and loved; the other, an educator and expert leadership consultant. For

Br. Joseph Schmidt, this beautiful little book is a fitting crown to a lifetime's devotion to Thérèse. For Marisa Guerin, it is a sharing of the heart qualities that illumine her own pilgrimage through life.

"We might be surprised to learn that so many of us in the twenty-first century can be helped by this nineteenth century French enclosed Carmelite nun whose own soul was so painfully forged on the anvil of tragedy and trauma. But Schmidt and Guerin are sensitive interpreters who use Thérèse's tortured complexity to present her as a credible mentor to those of us struggling today with brokenness and woundedness. *Life Lessons* offers us a moral compass to navigate our way out of the tangled labyrinths we get sucked into by our addictions and compulsions. Anyone who finishes this book will emerge with an unexpected serenity and inner peace that are grounded in the conviction that despite our fragility, each one of us is held tenderly in the unbreakable grip of God's Love."

—Fr. Eamonn Mulcahy, CSSp, is a Spiritan of the British Province who has had extensive experience in giving retreats to priests and religious.

"*Life Lessons from St. Thérèse of Lisieux* is an insightful and hope-filled journey through Thérèse's life. As a recovering perfectionist caught in the crossfire between external demands and internal expectations, I found her mentoring in the love of her Little Way to be wise, helpful, and encouraging. The book is a healing balm in our increasingly contentious and stress-filled world."

—Tim Fallon, President, TSI Consulting Partners, Inc., author of *What Jesus Said and Why It Matters Now*

Life Lessons

from

St. Thérèse of Lisieux

Joseph F. Schmidt, FSC

Marisa Guerin, PhD

theWORD among us® press

Published by The Word Among Us Press
7115 Guilford Drive, Suite 100
Frederick, Maryland 21704
wau.org

26 25 24 23 22   1 2 3 4 5

ISBN: 978-1-59325-615-9
eISBN: 978-1-59325-616-6

Cover design by Suzanne Earl

Library of Congress Control Number: 2022912875

Table of Contents

Preface

St. Thérèse of Lisieux might seem an unlikely choice for a life coach. From the outside, her story is probably much different from our own.

Thérèse Martin was born in Alençon, France, in 1873, the youngest of five daughters of Louis and Zélie Martin. She had a loving but complicated childhood, and when she was fifteen years of age, she entered the convent at the Carmel of Lisieux. After nine years as a Carmelite sister, Thérèse died of tuberculosis at the age of twenty-four. As her writings and life story became widely known, many people were blessed by her goodness. Thérèse was declared a saint in 1925, only twenty-eight years after her death.

Thérèse was a holy young woman, to be sure. But does it make sense to consider her a mentor for our lives today? Skepticism might be reasonable, but it would be a mistake to discount Thérèse.

In meeting Thérèse, we encounter a genuine paradox. On the one hand, she was an unpretentious, ordinary person. She led a hidden life in a cloistered convent in the late nineteenth century; she probably met fewer people in her whole life than a typical city dweller today encounters in a week. She had no scholarly training and experienced no heavenly apparitions. Thérèse left behind no big projects, no institutions, no famous works—nothing except her autobiographical notebooks, her many letters and poems, and the respect and affection of those who knew her.

On the other hand, this unaffected young woman displayed an original and penetrating understanding of the human heart. In her short lifetime, she attained a remarkable level of psychological and spiritual maturity. Beneath the surface of her kind and happy personality, Thérèse in her twenties had garnered exceptional emotional self-awareness and spiritual discernment. By reflecting on the day-to-day joyful and sorrowful experiences of her life, by pondering the Scriptures, and by absorbing the wisdom of others who had gone before, Thérèse gained a liberating vision of life.

In telling her own story, Thérèse provided a clear-eyed grasp of the inner dynamics of growing up, experiences that most people have had but not seriously respected. Thérèse knew firsthand about the early childhood hurts that can escape memory. She understood the adaptations and the behavioral habits that we turn to for psychic survival. She saw the ways we can make others into "enemies" and the emotionally damaging, unreasonable expectations we hold for ourselves and others in our unconscious quest for affirmation.

Thérèse's dreams, traumas, joys, and challenges were much like our own. Her experiences closely mirror our inner psychological realities. She is intimately familiar with the emotional landscape of the heart and the down-to-earth challenges of ordinary life. Thérèse is a life coach who "gets" us.

This paradoxical figure—Thérèse of Lisieux—has influenced the lives of millions, from popes to plain folks. Pope Pius X hailed her as "the greatest saint in modern times."

The life lessons we can take from Thérèse are especially relevant in today's turbulent times. That's not because she holds answers to policy issues in a troubled world; Thérèse doesn't directly address social dilemmas. Rather, through her personal experience of love, loss, trauma, and healing, Thérèse shows us what a mature person with a free and loving heart looks like. She offers us hope and confident guidance for a life of meaning, contentment, loving relationships, productive work, and service to others.

Thérèse dealt with her life circumstances as she found them, facing the weaknesses, vulnerabilities, and passionate desires of her heart with courage and unflinching honesty. In her story, perhaps to our surprise, we can find a kindred spirit. We invite you to get to know Thérèse as a mentor for restless hearts.

A Note for Readers

We have created a rhythm throughout this book between exploring the wisdom of St. Thérèse of Lisieux and considering how it connects with the lives of people today—with your life perhaps. In each chapter, we use Thérèse's own words to illustrate fundamental elements of the path that she came to call her "Little Way." In the second part of each chapter, we suggest mentoring messages that contemporary readers might take from the wisdom of Thérèse. We explore how these messages might come alive in today's world. Many of the examples we use come from real interactions, and others are composites of people and circumstances we know.

We have divided the book into two parts. Part I, "The Healing Vision of Thérèse of Lisieux," provides a brief biography and description of Thérèse's treasured vision. It includes information about her experience of freedom from childhood compulsions. It continues through her discovery of the true loving character of God, which awakened in her what human love is and what it is not, an awareness that released her from the bondage of perfectionism. Part I concludes with a description of her personal tendency to value self-reflection and self-awareness as indispensable for a life of meaning and love.

Part II explores in depth the six heart qualities that we identify as essential to Thérèse's Little Way: inner freedom, compassion, creativity, a willing spirit, gratefulness, and self-surrender. Although these heart qualities are interrelated, each chapter focuses on one particular quality as it arises within the trajectory of Thérèse's life experience. These six hallmarks of Thérèse's Little Way are markers of emotional health in the language of psychology. They are also the signal attributes of the spiritual maturity that we see in the life of Jesus and in the lives of other holy people.

Thérèse saw these heart qualities as signs that she was keeping on the path of love and away from violence toward herself or others. These qualities are closely compatible with the wisdom to be found in Twelve Step programs for persons in recovery from substance abuse and for their loved ones. They are the attributes of mature and resilient persons.

Most of the quotations in the text are from Thérèse's autobiography, *The Story of a Soul*; others are from her collected letters or her last conversations, as recorded by her companions. Thérèse's words are capitalized or italicized if they appear that way in her original writing. You will find repetition of some information and themes throughout this book, a necessary overlap as we consider Thérèse's life from various angles.

We anticipate that you may sense an inner resistance to Thérèse's use of flowery language and images. This use is simply a reflection of the time in which she lived. You might also find yourself resisting her concept of "littleness." Thérèse uses the imagery of being like a child, with words like "nothingness" and "littleness," to describe our reality as creatures before the mystery of God. This wording might seem dismissive to those who feel marginalized because of race or gender. But Thérèse isn't suggesting that anyone should be weak or unduly submissive. Far from it. She was a courageous, even stubborn, young woman who was willing to draw boundaries when necessary.

Finally, we sometimes use the word "compulsion" when discussing Thérèse's childhood experiences. It is a word she didn't use, but it reflects an aspect of her personality that resonates today in terms of behavioral development. Thérèse understood that her childhood inclination to always be perfect and good was a way of coping with her needs for love and connection to her family. She knew this tendency's power over her; she was unable to shake it on her own. Thérèse's "compulsion" in this regard corresponds with the broader contemporary use of that word, and so we use the term in this book.

Mentoring, Not Instruction

A mentor is not the same as a teacher, nor is a mentor a supervisor. A mentor is a trusted advisor who guides a less experienced person by coaching, example, and supportive relationship. The way Thérèse approached those she counseled corresponds well to this contemporary notion of mentoring.

Thérèse served as an unofficial novice mistress (for various reasons, Carmelite rules prohibited her official appointment), guiding new members of her convent community in their spiritual formation. In that role, Thérèse did not usually give others specific instructions to follow. She trusted that each person would have their own privileged way of growing into the attitudes of heart and mind that lead to an authentic, productive, and loving life. When she shared her insights, Thérèse was direct and at times passionate, but she advised others without scolding, preaching, or being judgmental. Her way of teaching models for us a deep respect for the unique interior life of every person.

When Thérèse mentored others, she offered something to reflect on, perhaps a different perspective. Thérèse's guidance created a space that allowed something within to shift and to grow. How might we take in her wisdom?

Rather than trying to apply an instruction, we recommend that you allow yourself to be open to the seeds planted by the mentoring messages and then simply be willing to be changed. We don't suggest working at developing the various heart qualities that we describe. Such a tight grip on the steering wheel of our personal growth is the signature of an ego that is not our fullest, best self.

Our desire for control can become coercive and oppressive. Our attitude toward our personal growth can become one of grasping and directing rather than welcoming, open, receiving, and participating in the journey of life. The tendency to seek control can even masquerade as a spiritual stance.

Thérèse's gift is her constant discovery of ways to avoid the violence to her own spirit or to others that inevitably results when self-centeredness takes over. Thérèse saw herself as the recipient of grace, of blessings that grew in her when she didn't let her own preferences block a situation.

A Pathway through This Book

This is a "come as you are" book. There isn't any preparation necessary other than curiosity and openness. Thérèse invites us to a journey that can change us from the inside out.

As we embark on this reflective venture, we may sense an invitation to sort through the deep hopes in our hearts. What is the yearning within us? What would a meaningful, peaceful, loving life look like? We don't have to imitate Thérèse exactly; in fact, we couldn't do that. Each of us has different gifts, limitations, and life circumstances. It is enough to reflect honestly on our own life in the light of the insights Thérèse shares with us and then to act with confidence.

Thérèse assures us that wherever we're starting from, it's the right place. We're not going to get this way of loving and living perfectly right, and that's okay. We needn't worry about whether we will stumble on this path of Thérèse's Little Way: *of course* we will!

We aren't perfect; nor was Thérèse. She assures us that she stumbled. Failure is just part of our truth as human persons with weaknesses. Embracing Thérèse's vision, we can realize that we are loved *precisely* in our inadequacy. As she wrote toward the end of her life, "I am simply resigned to see myself always imperfect and in this I find my joy."[1]

Thérèse's mentoring will help us live peacefully and compassionately with our own fragile selves and with others. We can learn to deal better with our life situations, summoning courage, creativity, and realism to walk our own little way.

Part I

The Healing
Vision
of
Thérèse of
Lisieux

Chapter 1

Thérèse and Her "Only Treasure"

Many people have heard of Thérèse of Lisieux by her formal name, Thérèse of the Child Jesus, or by her nickname, "The Little Flower." Some know her as the "Little Theresa," in comparison to the "Big Teresa" of Avila, the great Spanish saint of the seventeenth century. No matter how we know her—casually or in depth—Thérèse has become one of the most popular saints of the Catholic Church.

Thérèse of Lisieux was virtually our contemporary. She died in 1897; if she had lived to be ninety, an age that two of her older sisters reached, she would have lived until 1963. But Thérèse died at the young age of twenty-four, succumbing to tuberculosis. Most likely she would have died in anonymity, like countless good and holy people, if not for her writings and the help that her life and her teachings inspired in those who came to know of her.

Thérèse wrote her autobiography at the request of her superiors. After her death, the Carmelite sisters in France circulated the document, and it soon found a wide audience. The autobiography resonated with the life experiences of ordinary people, both lay and ordained, who were encouraged too by Thérèse's promise to do good on earth after her death. *The Story of a Soul* has now been translated into fifty-five languages and read by millions, along with Thérèse's published letters and other accounts of her life compiled by her companions.

Thérèse's life story and her letters give us special access to her childhood memories and her journey to adulthood. She writes candidly and perceptively, revealing her thoughtfulness and sense of humor. A gifted storyteller, Thérèse describes the adventures of her childhood in a loving and devout family. She recounts her few dismal years at a boarding school where she was a day student and the challenges she faced in fulfilling her vocation as a Carmelite, sharing many anecdotes of convent life.

Thérèse's autobiography is like an intimate conversation with a good friend. It reveals a young woman who is transparent; she doesn't "spin" her account. Her keen self-understanding comes through as she describes moments of grace and growth and also the occasional missteps and excesses that flowed from her passionate nature. She does her best to tell the truth of her experience, the painful parts as well as the blessings.

Thérèse writes, "I find myself at a period in my life when I can cast a glance on the past; my soul has matured in the crucible of exterior and interior trials."[2] From Thérèse's point of view, her memoir was the honest story of the ups and downs of her life, in which she saw the goodness of God at work. Referencing Psalm 88, she tells us, "I'm going to be doing only one thing: I shall begin to sing what I must sing eternally: *'The Mercies of the Lord.'*"[3]

Thérèse realized that she was not the center of her life. Rather, she lived at the center of God's mercy.

Some Characteristics of Thérèse's Personality

Thérèse's autobiography quickly corrects any impression that she was a docile, naïve weakling. Her personality was a singular blend of determination, sweetness, and sincere affection. But it can come as a surprise to discover that the saint was strong-willed and determined.

As a child, Thérèse threw tantrums that led her mother to think the girl might die of exasperation. In a letter to family members, her mother wrote, "I am obliged to correct this poor little baby who gets into frightful tantrums; when things don't go just right and according to her way of thinking, she rolls on the floor in desperation like one without any hope."[4]

Already Thérèse clearly exhibited a strong willfulness. "As for the little imp," her mother wrote, ". . . [she] has a stubborn streak in her that is almost invincible; when she says *'no'* nothing can make her give in, and one could put her in the cellar a whole day and she'd sleep there rather than say 'yes.'"[5]

As she grew, Thérèse learned to manage her feelings. The adult Thérèse displayed quiet force in standing her emotional ground when challenged.

Along with strength of will and resolve, Thérèse had a keen intellect and a good memory. She had only five years of formal education, was mostly homeschooled, and had no advanced education. She was a good student however, and she loved to read.

> I had always loved the great and the beautiful, but at this epoch in my life I was taken up with an extreme desire for learning. Not satisfied with the lessons and work my teacher was giving me, I applied myself to some special studies in *history* and *science*, and I did this on my own. . . . [I]n a few months I acquired more knowledge than during my years of study.[6]

Thérèse's desire for learning fed her love of nature and the world, which she saw as God's good creation.

Thérèse's father read to the family from the lives of the saints. And as an adult, Thérèse had access to the Gospels, the letters of St. Paul, and a few other religious texts. At the time, the Church discouraged Catholics from reading the entire Bible, deeming it too dense and incomprehensible for most. Fortunately, Thérèse avoided the sometimes dreadful "holy" books of her time, with their emphasis on God's wrath. Her spiritual wisdom came primarily from her lifelong practice of reflecting on her own life experience and interpreting it through the lens of the Scriptures that were available to her.

Thérèse had an unusually high degree of honesty, self-awareness, and psychological insight—gifts that had a significant impact on her growth. In her writing, she recounted that from a very young age, she could sense what was happening on the "inside" and how her feelings rushed to take over.

We know from Thérèse's story that her personal emotional development was a lifelong venture. She was deeply affected by early losses. Her mother died when Thérèse was only four, and older sisters—mother figures to the young Thérèse—eventually left home for the convent. These losses seemed to trigger in Thérèse a need for the praise and appreciation of others, which at times seemed compulsive. She was saved from the trap of codependence by a teenage experience she called her "complete conversion" (we'll describe that experience in the next chapter). This conversion freed her from ten years of bondage to moodiness and depression, feelings that had overcome her at the death of her mother.

Flowing from the transformative experience of her conversion, Thérèse's new inner freedom reconnected her to her childhood joy, playfulness, and spontaneity. She was released from her excessive sensitivity and the mild depression that drained her energy and gave the appearance that she had "no will but that of others."[7] She came to recognize that she could manage, even befriend, her feelings. Then, through her desire for God and her honest interactions with others, she grew into a more authentic way of relating.

Thérèse continued throughout her life to develop sensitive and honest self-awareness; simple, creative, and straightforward trust; and enduring patience with herself and others. A year after what she called her conversion, aware of her psychological and spiritual readiness, she entered the convent at Lisieux. In doing so, she overcame the objections of a number of Church officials, who thought she was too young. This was a remarkable accomplishment for a fifteen-year-old girl.

Thérèse's world within the walls of the convent was small, but it was an authentic microcosm of humanity. Within those walls, she faced the typical dynamics that arise in every community of real people: love and pain, petty squabbles, power politics, leader-member stresses, and a full gamut of personalities, including some members who were seriously disturbed. In fact, a cloistered community may have been an especially challenging place for her to live a loving life since there was no escape from the feelings stirred by these lifetime companions whom she had not chosen. No matter how well-intentioned and committed to holiness, they were all flawed human beings.

Thérèse was devout and serious in her commitment to religious life, but she was anything but dour. Her novice mistress, Sr. Marie of the Angels, described her as witty and a great mimic: "She can make you weep with devotion and just as easily split your sides with laughter during recreations."[8] Thérèse kept her times of struggle to herself and did her best to be a helpful and friendly member of the community.

Thérèse's mature tranquility gradually attracted the respect of the other sisters. Only on reading her autobiography after her death did the sisters realize that, beneath Thérèse's kind and even temperament, she suffered severely in some community interactions. As we will see in later chapters, there were times when she felt bullied, confused, misunderstood, or disrespected; yet she bore her inner sensitivities with peace and patience.

Thérèse's life story shows us a strong-willed child, an avid learner, a girl who struggled with depression, and a young adult who was committed to a loving life within a religious vocation. To the people who knew her best during her lifetime, Thérèse came across as a kind person who coped with typical emotional gifts and limitations as she matured. They saw her as one of them. Some may well have been surprised had they been told that Thérèse was to be named a saint and later a master of the spiritual life for the whole Catholic Church.

A Spiritual Teacher

Many people who become saints are scholars, martyrs, founders of religious orders, or some other type of notable religious figure. Their biographies often feature stories of heroism and miraculous events. Thérèse could claim none of these sources of credibility. And yet in 1997, one hundred years after her death, the Vatican took the extraordinary step of naming St. Thérèse a Doctor of the Church.

Doctors of the Church are canonized saints and often scholars who have made significant contributions to the teaching of the Church. At the time Thérèse was so designated, there were fewer than three dozen Doctors out of many hundreds of saints. Almost all of them were men, such as St. Thomas Aquinas, St. Augustine, and St. Jerome. Thérèse is not only the youngest Doctor of the Church, but she is also the closest to us in time.

The apostolic letter proclaiming Thérèse's new title referred to her as "a living icon of that God who . . . shows his almighty power in his mercy and forgiveness."[9] With the authority of the Vatican, this letter validates for Christians Thérèse's status as a master of the spiritual life. The proclamation goes on to affirm that Thérèse offers a mature synthesis of Christian spirituality, combining theology and the spiritual life and expressed with strength, authority, and particular originality.

Thérèse's standing as a Doctor of the Church means that her teaching is squarely within the Catholic tradition and faithful to the developing understanding of the gospel. This is a testimony to the authenticity of her insights, which were often cutting-edge or even contrary to the prevailing religious views of her times—and sometimes of ours.

Significantly, the Vatican proclamation highlights the fact that Thérèse brings to the Church's teaching the sensibilities of a woman. The feminine perspective was, and remains, largely missing from most theological writing. Thérèse's teaching flows naturally from her life experience as a woman, a daughter, a sister. The proclamation document also points out the even rarer fact of Thérèse's youth. Her writing is infused with the freshness, hope, joy, and playfulness of a young person.

Thérèse's status as a Doctor of the Church begs the questions: What was notable about what she taught? Why is she so significant, despite the absence of the exceptional external accomplishments that were characteristic of most of the Doctors? Thérèse stands out in two ways: her message and her method.

The essence of Thérèse's message was nothing less than a rediscovery for the modern world of the original gospel message of mercy, love, and healing. Thérèse's teaching arose at a time when many were in need of liberation from the grip of harsh, punitive, false ideas about God's justice and wrath. Despite the lack of regular access to spiritual direction or theological training, Thérèse came to live and teach a way of daily creative love, without doing violence to oneself, to others, or to the world.

Thérèse offers a universal message: no one can live in peace without knowing they are loveable and loved. Thérèse grasped this truth; further, she became aware of the powerful connection between how we manage our feelings and our ability to live a peaceful, loving life. Her sophisticated understanding of the dynamics of our inner life is one of the reasons she is considered a modern saint. Instead of locating the source of holiness in penances or sacrifices that we might perform, Thérèse shows us that the treasure is waiting within us, in our patient acceptance of our human limitations and our willingness to welcome God's unfailing love into our hearts.

From Thérèse we learn that living a good life is not payment for a ticket to heaven; rather, a loving life of service and justice unfolds as our free and grateful response to the overwhelming generosity of God's great love for us. This represents a radical change for many believers. By overturning our assumptions about what God expects of us, Thérèse corrects grim, fear-based interpretations of religious teaching and reveals the joy that is the essence of the gospel.

Thérèse is also notable as a modern teacher of the spiritual life because of her deceptively simple method. This centered on her capacity for perceptive reflection on her life as it unfolded. In other words, Thérèse was closely attuned to the daily ups and downs of her life. When she paid careful attention to her experience of a situation, she attended not only to the outside event but especially to the internal aspects of what the event was doing to her.

In many cases, there was nothing of real note in an external situation; it could have been just a brief conversation or a casual remark. The moment turned out to be important for Thérèse because of the internal feelings it generated within her—emotions like anxiety, joy, anger, or longing—and the insights that arose as she observed her own heart. In much the same way that people today seek self-understanding through psychotherapy, spiritual direction, or journaling, Thérèse probed her reflections in light of the lives and wisdom of others and through the lens of the Gospels and the teachings of St. Paul.

Through her regular process of reflection, Thérèse was able to gain extraordinary self-awareness. She befriended her feelings, allowing them to awaken her to what was true about her present experience and how it might connect with what was true about her past. This process was especially revealing for Thérèse because her point of view was that of a "little" one. This was her word for someone who is ordinary as opposed to someone who thinks they have all the answers. She courageously sought the truth, no matter how it arose or where it led. In the process, she was willing to drop defenses, extend her comfort zone, and notice blind spots. In short, she was willing to die to herself—to her self-centeredness and self-defensiveness—and rise to a higher level.

Thérèse's message and her method are gifts for us. Her writings and the testimony of those who knew her reveal a keenly perceptive young woman with the ability to translate her insights into action. With growing confidence, Thérèse taught others this authentic gospel message of love, untainted by the harsh vision of religion that was prevalent in her day.

Discovering Her "Only Treasure"

Thérèse's way is not flashy, but it is authentically human; it heals and encourages. The core of her wisdom Thérèse called her "only treasure," as in her correspondence with her sister Marie.

Marie wrote a letter to Thérèse expressing her hope that someday she might also have great thoughts like the ones that she assumed were Thérèse's gift. Thérèse responded by gently puncturing Marie's exalted notion of Thérèse's holiness. She assured Marie that she, Thérèse, was not at all unique. She encouraged Marie to reflect on her own life and discover these same gifts.

Thérèse went on to make a deeper point in her letter. Turning away from talk of great gifts, Thérèse spoke of her frank awareness that she, like everyone, was weak and imperfect. And *at the same time*, this awareness of her limitations and flaws was completely enfolded in her unfailing hope in the love of God.

To understand Thérèse, it is crucial to see that these two truths—her limitations and God's mercy—were always paired. The awareness of her imperfections *and* her confidence in God's love for her were a single reality. This is what she described to Marie as her "only treasure." She wrote, "What pleases Him is *that He sees me loving my littleness* and my *poverty, the blind hope that I have in His mercy. . . . That is my only treasure.*"[10]

What Thérèse meant by her "littleness and poverty" was her awareness of the great gap between the intense yearnings of her heart and the plain reality of her human weakness and inadequacies. She knew that on her own, she would never be able to live up to her desire for perfect goodness.

This inner poverty of spirit was a painful truth to face. But Thérèse was nothing if not bravely honest. Her acceptance and embrace of her limitations were not self-deprecation. She was not dodging her adult responsibilities or taking refuge in false humility. Acknowledging her littleness and poverty was her way of truthfully naming her basic humanness, her absolute dependence on God.

Thérèse's words identifying her "only treasure" sum up the core of her spiritual vision: first, her loving acceptance of her human, imperfect self and, second, a welcoming hope in the love and mercy of the mystery she knew as God. These two elements taken together, this "only treasure," was radically freeing for Thérèse, bearing fruit in her life of love.

Thérèse believed that hers was a treasure that everyone could have. Like Thérèse, we have hearts that are restless and yearning for love. Like Thérèse, we can be harshly judged by our inner critic, often disappointed in ourselves. What Thérèse was sharing with her sister Marie then, and with us now, is a fundamental message. It is the twofold truth that we will always be imperfect, yet at the same time, we can trust that we are held securely in the embrace of the infinitely loving God.

Thérèse concluded her letter to Marie with these words, encouraging to Marie and to all seekers of peace: "Why would this treasure not be yours?"[11]

Indeed, why would this treasure not be ours?

Mentoring Messages for Reflection

The ordinary nature of Thérèse's way reassures us. In her life story, we find two messages that shape our perspective: first, an awareness that what matters most about our lives starts on the inside, in our reflective hearts, and, second, a realization that the wholly loving nature of God brings us freedom and peace.

✧ A meaningful, joyful life is an "inside job"; our worldly accomplishments are not the point.

Thérèse's genius lay in her penetrating understanding of the human heart. Her vision assures us that—in a certain and ultimate sense—it doesn't matter how big or small our life accomplishments are in the eyes of the world. Living a life of love is essentially an "inside" job.

While it is a privilege to impact society through work as a physician, an educator, a CEO, or a political leader, Thérèse affirms that it can be just as fulfilling and just as worthy to be a devoted partner, a caring parent, a good neighbor, a small business owner, a worker, or a student. The key to a meaningful and peaceful life, in the final analysis, is not in what we do but in how we live. As Thérèse's example shows us, the life of a kind and loving person reaches out like ripples on a lake, bringing goodness, justice, and blessing to the world—sometimes in quiet, unseen ways.

The critical "inside" element in living a meaningful life is the capacity for honest reflection on our experience. Thérèse's reflective approach is readily available to ordinary people like us because it's an intuitive process; it arises naturally. We think about our lives whether we want to or not, often replaying some feeling or moment over and over. We mull over the remark we made or failed to make; the anxiety we feel about finding a good job, meeting that special someone, or how things are going at work. Thérèse teaches us not to run a worry cycle but rather to consider such questions as, What is going on inside me? What do my feelings show me about myself?

It is in thoughtful, reflective times that we gain insight, the glimpse that reveals our deeper need or our personal agenda. This is true even if our time for reflection has to be creatively braided into the busy routines of home and work.

Our second mentoring message for this chapter concerns Thérèse's understanding of God's wholly loving nature.

✧ The loving and nonviolent nature of God allows us a freedom that changes everything.

In Thérèse's time, the question about how to live a good life kept many people worried, guilt-ridden, and striving to be perfect. They feared lest a punitive God send them to eternal damnation. Even today, when fewer people are explicitly religious, the dynamics of anxiety, self-condemnation, and perfectionism live in many hearts.

Some of us have been raised to fear the harsh and judgmental God whom people dreaded in Thérèse's day. Others have internalized the high expectations of parents or the wider society and live under the tyranny of their inner critic. Whatever the source, the result can be the same: we inflict the violence of perfectionism on ourselves.

Thérèse's vision represents a definitive break with this suffering. Her way is securely based on a crucially important insight: that God, especially as manifest by Jesus in the Gospels, is merciful, loving, and not violent in any way. For Thérèse, this was an intuitive leap, a direct, transformative insight. Trusting that we are held securely in God's all-encompassing love and that God *never* relates to us cruelly was, for Thérèse, a radical awareness.

A nonviolent, nonadversarial, loving stance toward ourselves, toward others, and toward life is the defining characteristic of Thérèse's psychological and spiritual vision and of her way. The source of Thérèse's joy was her conviction that she was loved just as she was. This bedrock trust in the unfailing love of God can be a healing perspective for us as well, dissolving the inner perfectionist who so much wants to live a good life but collapses in the suffering that comes from the violence of self-blame.

Thérèse's "only treasure" is a perspective that can change everything.

Although the gospel message of the essentially loving nature of God is a pervasive theme in Thérèse's teaching, "love without violence" may be an unfamiliar lens through which to view her Little Way. This perspective challenges many mistaken and distorted assumptions about God, and it offers a way of living in today's world that is subtly countercultural. Thérèse's message of love without violence is woven throughout this book.

Chapter 2

Freeing the Captive

All of us have needy hearts and inner wounds, and we develop patterns of coping with our hurts as we become adults. Some of these patterns cripple our capacity to develop into fully mature persons. But these patterns protect us too. In this chapter, we will focus on one pivotal moment on Thérèse's path to maturity that planted the seeds for her own profound experience of inner liberation from the childhood compulsions that held sway in her.

The incident happened when Thérèse was a teenager; she called it her "complete conversion." When Thérèse used the word "conversion," she wasn't using it the way we are accustomed to hearing it—namely, as a reference to the moment when we accept a religious faith. Thérèse was a devout Catholic from childhood; her "complete conversion" was not a cognitive assent to a set of beliefs. Rather, it was a profound psychological and deeply spiritual event, a definitive, life-changing moment that flowed from her capacity for truthful self-awareness. It started her on the path of liberation and healing from the wounds of her childhood.

Thérèse described this conversion as an *interior* experience, something that no one else had noticed at the time, except her sister Céline. As a brilliant illumination of Thérèse's heart and as a striking empowerment of her will, her conversion rescued her from excessive reliance on the approval of others and set her on a course of inner freedom and authenticity. Its transformative power grew within her for the rest of her life, as she gradually came to understand its layers of meaning.

Childhood Hurts and Unmanaged Feelings

To understand the roots of the false way of living that fell away in the moment of Thérèse's complete conversion, it might help to look at her earliest years.

Thérèse's mother, Zélie Martin, was ill with the early stages of breast cancer when Thérèse was born. For the baby's survival, Zélie had to entrust the three-month-old Thérèse to Rose Taillé, a young mother who served as a wet nurse. Baby Thérèse stayed with Rose and her family, living on the Taillé farm just outside the city of Alençon until she was weaned.

Rose's family were farmers, so Rose came once a week to buy and sell produce in the market in Alençon. On those days, she left the infant Thérèse with her birth family. This back-and-forth routine continued for nine months. When the infant Thérèse was returned to her family for good, Thérèse suffered the loss of the one she knew as her "first" mother, Rose.

Then, only three years later, Zélie succumbed to cancer, and Thérèse's world fell apart. Feeling alone and abandoned, she retreated into herself. Remembering this sad time as she wrote her autobiography years later, Thérèse was honest about its effect on her:

> My happy disposition completely changed after Mama's death. I, once so full of life, became timid and retiring, sensitive to an excessive degree. One look was enough to reduce me to tears, and the only way I was content was to be left alone completely. I could not bear the company of strangers and found my joy only within the intimacy of the family.[12]

In the years after her mother's death, Thérèse lost her childhood cheerfulness, sociability, and unbounded liveliness. She suffered a mild, pervasive depression, a complicated grief that did not resolve. She wrote, "I was really unbearable because of my extreme touchiness."[13]

Grasping for the security of permanent bonding, Thérèse rushed to adopt her sixteen-year-old sister Pauline as her new mother, declaring, "Well, as for me, it's Pauline who will be my Mama!"[14] Pauline had already bonded with Thérèse as caregiver and teacher, and now she became a special confidante. She assured Thérèse of her fidelity and spiritual companionship. With Pauline at her side, Thérèse felt that she would never be abandoned and that the two of them would someday walk together into religious life.

When Thérèse was nine years old, however, Pauline, without much warning to Thérèse, left for the Carmelite convent in Lisieux. Reflecting later on this painful moment, Thérèse wrote, "If I had learned of my dear Pauline's departure very gently, I would not have suffered as much perhaps, but having heard about it by surprise, it was as if a sword were buried in my heart."[15] Thérèse had lost another "mother." "How can I express the anguish of my heart!" she wrote.[16]

Thérèse tried desperately to maintain some connection to Pauline during brief convent visits, but it didn't work. "I ended up by recognizing the sad reality: Pauline is lost to me, almost in the same manner as if she were dead."[17]

Heartbroken and shaken, Thérèse turned more completely to her father and her other sisters. In the affectionate language of the family, Thérèse's father was her King, and she was his little Queen. Thérèse was indulged in her role as the favorite of her father and sweetheart of everyone. She of course did not resist being pampered.

Nevertheless, Thérèse continued to suffer from her unmanaged feelings. She went on to experience several frightening nightmares as well as illnesses that the doctors were unable to diagnose, signals of her emotional fragility. Her family assumed that she would grow out of the excessive sensitivity that seemed to drain her willpower.

Thérèse's Conversion, in Her Own Words

Less than two weeks before Thérèse's fourteenth birthday, she had the experience that she called her "complete conversion." This unexpected and decisive event not only exposed and released her from her moodiness and sensitivity, but it also revealed the hidden violence in this thinking and behavior. She was conscious of its impact for the rest of her life. She recalled:

> God would have to work a little miracle to make me *grow up* in an instant, and this miracle He performed on that unforgettable Christmas day. On that luminous *night* which sheds such light on the delights of the Holy Trinity, Jesus, the gentle, *little* Child of only one hour, changed the night of my soul into rays of light.
>
> On that *night* when He made Himself subject to *weakness* and suffering for love of me, He made me *strong* and courageous, arming me with His weapons. Since that night I have never been defeated in any combat, but rather walked from victory to victory, beginning, so to speak, *"to run as a giant"*! (Psalm 18:6)[18]

Here she recounts the experience of that Christmas night:

> It was December 25, 1886, that I received the grace of leaving my childhood, in a word, the grace of my complete conversion. We had come back from Midnight Mass where I had the happiness of receiving the *strong* and *powerful* God. Upon arriving at Les Buissonnets, I used to love to take my shoes from the chimney corner and examine the presents in them; this old custom had given us so much joy in our youth that Céline wanted to continue treating me as a baby since I was the youngest in the family.
>
> Papa had always loved to see my happiness and listen to my cries of delight as I drew each surprise from the *magic shoes*, and my dear King's gaiety increased my own happiness

very much. However, Jesus desired to show me that I was to give up the defects of my childhood and so He withdrew its innocent pleasures. He permitted Papa, tired out after the Midnight Mass, to experience annoyance when seeing my shoes at the fireplace, and that he speak those words which pierced my heart: "Well, fortunately, this will be the last year!"

I was going upstairs, at the time, to remove my hat, and Céline, knowing how sensitive I was and seeing the tears already glistening in my eyes, wanted to cry too, for she loved me very much and understood my grief. She said, "Oh, Thérèse, don't go downstairs; it would cause you too much grief to look at your slippers right now!" But Thérèse was no longer the same; Jesus had changed her heart!

Forcing back my tears, I descended the stairs rapidly; controlling the poundings of my heart, I took my slippers and placed them in front of Papa, and withdrew all the objects joyfully. I had the happy appearance of a Queen. Having regained his own cheerfulness, Papa was laughing; Céline believed it was all a *dream*! Fortunately, it was a sweet reality; Thérèse had discovered once again the strength of soul which she had lost at the age of four and a half, and she was to preserve it forever![19]

The Inner Drama

Within the story of what happened on that memorable evening, we can discern the features of a dramatic internal shift, giving birth to an inner freedom that surged in Thérèse from that moment on.

The stage was set as Thérèse came home from church on Christmas Eve with her father and her older sister Céline. Even though all three of them privately knew that she was actually too old for such childish customs, Thérèse was looking forward to the traditional children's ritual. As she went up the stairs to take off her hat, the words of her father, tired and irritable after the lengthy church service, thrust Thérèse into the world of failure. Her father was disappointed in his little Queen! The rejection Thérèse felt went straight to the core of her being. Tears came to her eyes.

But Thérèse didn't cry. She felt something shift within her. She saw herself differently, and she was, in fact, different. "Thérèse was no longer the same." She discovered that she didn't need to resist or flee from her feelings, that she could bear her feelings of being imperfect.

By sheer grace, Thérèse received in that instant of clarity the strength to let go of the illusion of who she thought she was. For the first time in her life, that flash of deep consciousness brought to her mind the certainty that the acceptable, loving people pleaser who made a disturbance over the least thing was *not* her real identity. Thérèse experienced the gift of self-awareness and inner strength.

Céline, observing that Thérèse had overheard her father's words, assumed that her sister would feel upset, and she wanted to comfort her. But to Céline's astonishment, Thérèse exhibited a new inner strength. She stood her emotional ground and stepped away from taking her father's words as her only truth. Yes, her heart was wounded; but with awareness and self-control, Thérèse composed herself and kept her feelings of distress from overpowering her. She didn't blame anybody; she didn't turn away from her father in fear or mistrust. And Thérèse didn't criticize herself.

"Forcing back my tears" and "controlling the poundings of my heart," Thérèse came back downstairs and turned a stressed moment into a happy Christmas Eve. She cheered her tired father as she performed the usual childhood ritual. Céline thought it was a miracle!

For Thérèse, this was the moment that pierced the psychological shield she had built and carried. Instead of a meltdown, she had a transformation, and she would be grateful for this grace for the rest of her life. At this pivotal moment, everything was the same for Thérèse, and everything was different. From the outside, she was still a loving and loveable sweetheart, as pleasing in her actions as before. Her father actually noticed nothing different. But on the inside, Thérèse experienced a complete change.

In that charged moment, Thérèse was brought home to herself; she accepted her integrity, self-respect, and true self. It was a genuine moment of self-awareness; no new game was being played. She didn't force herself to let go of the hurt or by strength of will create a new self. Empowered by a sense of her own inner freedom, she saw herself consciously sustained by God's power, loved for who she was.

Thérèse experienced this power as mercy, and this mercy she knew to be God. From the awareness that came to her in the moment of her conversion, Thérèse started on a path of personal awareness, confident behavior, emotional resilience, and self-compassion.

The Terrible Fault and the Hidden Lie

There may have been even more to Thérèse's experience of her complete conversion. In her autobiography, she wrote that as a child, she had tried to practice virtue by pleasing God and helping Céline. At the same time, she noticed that she was unbearable because of her extreme touchiness, crying if her kind actions were not noticed and crying *again* for having cried in the first place. "All arguments were useless," she wrote. "I was quite unable to correct this terrible fault."[20]

Why would Thérèse think that this fault deserved to be registered as "terrible"? And what was she was unable to do?

Thérèse recognized that she had a problem, a serious fault that needed healing if she were ever to grow to maturity. She seems to have glimpsed not only that her behavior was immature but also that within the behavior was a hidden lie. She was not being truly honest when she saw herself as immature. She realized that her behavior served her neediness.

Furthermore, Thérèse had an intuition that she was bullying herself in her efforts to be pleasing. In striving to be good and even perfect, she was violating her authenticity, being untrue to herself. She was living in the grip of a lie. What was terrible about the lie and the self-bullying was that these were acts of violence toward herself.

Thérèse realized that her strenuous efforts to be pleasing and charming were ways of putting herself in charge of her life. She was not welcoming her life as a gift and mystery from God. She was not cultivating her life with creativity and honesty.

She was under the control of her ego, suffering the exhaustion and emptiness that come from acting out a false self.

It was her inability to break free of this pattern from childhood that Thérèse refers to when writing, "The work I had been unable to do in ten years was done by Jesus in one instant, contenting himself with my *good will* which was never lacking."[21] As she understood this graced moment, it was her willingness to stay in God's arms and not be enslaved by her feelings that allowed her to be truly free and loving. She glimpsed the bigger truth of her life, not the partial truths that had controlled her to that point. She realized that she could be aware of her feelings and that she had the inner power to freely respond to them.

In later years, Thérèse still had to cope with the compulsion to please others at the risk of violating her integrity. She was transformed by the grace of her powerful conversion experience but did not permanently gain her inner freedom; no one ever does. Thérèse was no longer dominated by her feelings, but she would always be sensitive to the reactions of others.

Thérèse's complete conversion was not only a psychological breakthrough but also a pivotal experience of spiritual healing. It marked a profound development in her spiritual maturity. In that graced moment, Thérèse saw that what she had thought was her failure was no barrier at all to God's merciful and healing love. Her spirituality changed from one that rested on *belief*—statements about the faith that she was personally responsible to fulfill—to one based on *trust*, knowing herself to be safe in God's loving arms. She was now on the path that would become her Little Way.

Mentoring Messages for Reflection

How does such an intensely personal memory for Thérèse translate into guidance for us? The layers within Thérèse's conversion are broadly universal. Her mentoring connects to our shared human experiences of woundedness, the mysterious ways in which healing happens, and the private nature of our inner life.

✧ We are not alone; having a wounded heart is part of life.

Our own childhood wounds may be different from Thérèse's, but we all have needy hearts. In the same way that Thérèse used her personal gifts to secure the affection of her family, we may have learned to use our smarts, a clever sense of humor, or other gifts to extract the love and approval that we need from others. Like Thérèse, we might find ourselves surviving emotionally by adapting in a way that is at odds with our deeper truth. The older we get, the more this adaptation causes strain within us. We aren't truly at home in ourselves, and we can't put our finger on what is wrong.

The good news is that our hearts seek wholeness and healing.

✧ A sense of freedom and healing may arise in us in ordinary graced moments.

Thérèse experienced liberation in a very ordinary way: she received this grace in a private, inner moment in the course of regular life. This should encourage us. Perhaps we have experienced a similar event, a moment in which we were given the grace to see clearly the truth of our lives. It may have happened in a conversation with a loved one or a trusted friend, or through a relationship with a helpful therapist, or during a time of reflective retreat.

An important inner shift in our awareness might also arise unexpectedly, at a point when we are primed to glimpse what is going on in us. In a flash of clarity, we may see what is behind our behavior or the unresolved pain that has a hold on our spirit. However, a sudden moment of revelation isn't necessary. It's probably more common that we sense a gradually dawning resilience in our spirit that grows stronger over time.

The incidents that offer us important self-awareness might be quite simple. One friend tells about riding in a car, conversing with a colleague. At a certain point in their exchange, the colleague turned to him and asked, "Do you realize how critical that sounds?"

It was a simple question, but it penetrated deeply. The truth was, our friend did *not* realize it; his eyes were opened. In recognizing the truth of this single observation, he also glimpsed the larger truth, an awareness of a need within him to control, to be in charge. As he reflected further on this awareness, it led him to greater freedom.

When something strikes us deeply, the "noticing" is a moment of grace. It gives us a glimpse into the subtle patterns that we have developed over time to protect our vulnerability. Even without a special illuminating event, we all have days when we realize that we aren't ourselves and don't act from our best selves. We regret what we do and feel the capacity to change, to be freed. We do our best, as Thérèse did—not always successfully but with patience and awareness of new possibilities for our life.

Thérèse's story teaches us that we can't *force* ourselves to be better persons. Her example is a counterweight to cultural messages that tell us we can succeed in our wishes by the sheer strength of our determination. The journey to freedom and wisdom is an inner process, often invisible to others. This informs another life lesson.

✧ Since our motives are invisible to others, sometimes the free choice to be loving can appear to be unfree.

The story of her conversion holds an important clue to the puzzle of how Thérèse often is misunderstood as a softhearted, nice-at-all-costs young woman. Her conversion was clearly a life-altering experience but also one that was invisible to anyone but herself. From an outsider's perspective, nothing changed; but on the inside, everything changed.

Thérèse's experience reminds us that it's not possible to know, from the outside, another person's motives or experience. Her complete conversion freed Thérèse from bondage to a false pattern of living. And yet freed, she proceeded to act in ways that, for all anyone knew, were pretty much the same as before. She continued to be kind, she was affectionate to her father and sisters, she was obedient and caring. The crucial difference was internal: Thérèse now made *choices* to act lovingly toward others.

Most of the time, the kindness that flows from our inner freedom will be visible only to ourselves. We alone will notice that we have held back the cutting comeback to the family member who is irritating us. No one will track that we have gotten better at checking our impulse to rush on to the next thing: instead of hurrying by, we might take a few minutes for a friendly greeting and a bit of conversation with a lonely neighbor. An outsider will not know the inner reality of our motivation if we put in an extra-long day at work; our labor could look like the action of a workaholic, compulsive personality rather than a free choice flowing from our desire to lovingly support someone else's situation.

There is no real need to draw attention to our behavior or our reasons, especially if we are trying to act from a heart that is free from the approval or disapproval of others. We have learned from Thérèse that what matters is our openness to acting confidently and lovingly from a free heart. Thérèse's story teaches us not to judge the motives of others, and it invites us to deeper reflection on our own motives.

Chapter 3

Resurrecting the God of Love

Thérèse's conversion crystallized for her a radical idea about the nature of God, an idea that she had intuited all along. Her insight was this: grounded in her unshakeable confidence that God is not violent, even to sinners, we can trust that God's love will always be creative and never be punitive or cruel. God is *always* on our side.

Thérèse, of course, had been taught about God's love as part of her religious upbringing. The Christmas gift of her conversion was to personally realize that God held her tenderly, as a parent caresses a small child, even in her failings. Her conversion didn't happen in her head but in the very center of her being; it gave her a glimpse into the heart of God, where she saw nothing but mercy.

Thérèse's insight into the merciful, never violent nature of God is profoundly significant in her teaching.

Knowing the True God

A spiritual framing of her life experience came naturally to Thérèse, raised as she was in a devout religious family. Throughout her life, she maintained a highly personal, intimate image of God, even during her painful final years, when she felt plunged into the darkest doubt. When Thérèse spoke of God, she was not referring to the common cultural image of a bearded, almighty, all-knowing, overpowering man in the sky—Someone who is a judge, ruler, and enforcer. Instead, she knew God as the One whom Jesus called "Father."

Because Thérèse was a beloved child of loving parents, who forgave and held no grudges, this gospel image of a loving Father-God resonated with her. As she grew up, her images of her relationship with God echoed her confidence and trust in the caring of her family, especially her close relationship with her father after her mother's death. From the psalms and other passages in the Bible, Thérèse noticed some violent images of God. Yet she believed that Jesus—who lived, taught, and died without violence to others—revealed most truly and compellingly what God is like: the transcendent vastness of Love that is always immediately present to us, beyond what anyone could ever imagine, an infinity of mercy. Thérèse grasped in the intimacy of her heart the gospel message about the goodness of God.

This view of God's loving nature was confirmed for her in Jesus' words: "If you then, who are wicked, know how to give good gifts to your children, how much more will your heavenly Father give good things to those who ask him" (Matthew

7:11). Thérèse came to understand that if we viewed God as violent and vindictive, then we accepted behavior on God's part that we would never accept in a good human parent. One of her favorite Scripture passages was the story of the forgiving father who joyfully welcomed the return of his chastened prodigal son (see Luke 15:11–32).

Other favorites included the humble prayer of the publican, which God graciously received (see Luke 18:9-14). And Thérèse came to understand that the God who sends the gift of rain upon the just and the unjust alike is the God who loves even an enemy (Matthew 5:45). She saw the God who cares about the good and bad, the rich and poor, the powerful and weak—everyone, and all of creation. Thérèse's understanding of the nature of God simply and convincingly derives from the good news of the loving God preached by Jesus.

This nonviolent God had all but died in the Middle Ages, on the battlefields of the Crusades. The Judeo-Christian tradition is long, and believers in successive eras have understood the faith story and the Scriptures differently, seeing them through the lens of their contemporary reality and with the inspiration of the Spirit. Thérèse, in her wisdom, came to see that the gospel message of God's loving mercy had been damaged by ideas that represented God as harsh and vengeful. These notions were firmly planted in the popular spiritual preaching and writings of her time.

This distorted understanding of God's nature had been formally condemned by the Church as the heresy known as Jansenism. But Jansenist thinking continued to poison the spirituality of Thérèse's time, and it persists in our own era. This fear-filled notion has alienated many people from religion. Thérèse's writings authoritatively confront such teachings and clarify the loving nature of God.

Thérèse Challenged Three Damaging Concepts about God

Thérèse's confidence that God is merciful and not vengeful provides the entire foundation of her Little Way. The clarity with which she saw the gospel image of a loving God led her to challenge three damaging notions that have prevailed in religious teaching and cultural attitudes.

The first of these mistaken ideas is that God is like a powerful ancient king whose justice takes the form of swift, harsh retaliation against wrongdoers. The second misconception is that human justice, modeled on this false understanding of God's justice, is primarily about punishment, retribution, and even revenge. The third misunderstanding of the gospel message is the notion that to avoid such harsh punishments, it is necessary to become morally excellent—and furthermore, that we are responsible to achieve this moral perfection through our own efforts.

Thérèse recognized that violence was the fundamental mistake lacing every aspect of these portrayals of God. These ideas set up the notion that God legitimates and approves of our violence too, as we blame, strive, judge, and punish ourselves and others, all to "earn" moral perfection. Society's justifications for "good violence" are built on these false beliefs.

God's Justice

The first damaging idea rejected by Thérèse has to do with how we understand God's justice. For many people, God's justice is more or less equivalent to the idea of being judged and punished for our offenses. The proclamation making Thérèse a Doctor of the Church specifically points out that she helped heal souls of the burden of feeling they were under God's wrath. The Church underlines the fact that Thérèse correctly understood the essence of the gospel: God doesn't hold grudges.

> [S]he helped to heal souls of the rigors and fears of Jansenism, which tended to stress God's justice rather than his divine mercy. . . . Thus she became a living icon of that God who, according to the Church's prayer, "shows his almighty power in his mercy and forgiveness" (cf. *Roman Missal*, Opening Prayer, 26th Sunday in Ordinary Time).[22]

All God's attributes, Thérèse wrote, are wrapped in mercy:

> Even His Justice . . . seems to me clothed in *love*. What a sweet joy it is to think that God is *Just*, i.e., that He takes into account our weakness, that He is perfectly aware of our fragile nature. What should I fear then? Ah! Must not the infinitely just God, who deigns to pardon the faults of the prodigal son with so much kindness, be just also toward me who "am with him always"?[23]

In her confidence that God is merciful, Thérèse wasn't implying that there is no such thing as wrongdoing or that her actions didn't matter. She grieved that there were countless times when she failed to be kind, when she put self-centeredness ahead of compassion or gave in to an intemperate mood or a selfish wish. Later in life, as she mentored others, Thérèse was careful not to imply that the unfailing love of God was some kind of free pass that would relieve us of our responsibility to choose the good. Rather, knowing God as a loving parent, she saw herself running straight into God's forgiving arms, penitent and trusting in God's mercy, not harshly condemning herself for being less than perfect.

Glimpsing the infinite horizon of God's love for us, Thérèse saw that God's justice desires that *all* of us have what we need for growth and that God is especially concerned with the poor and vulnerable. God is merciful to the just and the unjust, the offended as well as the offender, victim and victimizer alike. In short, God's justice is larger than human justice, beyond our notions of what is fair and necessary.

God's justice does *not retaliate*. God does not need to get back at us for our mistakes and sins. Nor does God need to restore God's dignity, as if it could be offended by our faults.

God's justice is not concerned with "balancing the books," as if evil actions were to be offset by good ones. Thérèse used gentle humor to correct this view among the sisters she counseled: "There is a science that He doesn't know: arithmetic!"[24] God's justice does not require us to "pay" for our bad actions, item by item.

Great numbers of Christians still think of God as a stern father who required the crucifixion of Jesus, his only Son, to assure that humanity's debt would be paid. This is a horrifying idea that didn't make sense to Thérèse. Her own father was a kind and loving man; God could be no less. Despite her lack of access to advanced biblical and theological studies, Thérèse discerned the fallacy that led people to conclude that God was no better than a murderer.

Instead of seeing God as a fearsome judge demanding blood sacrifice from his own Son, Thérèse understood that Jesus freely submitted himself to execution at the hands of Roman and religious authorities. He was willing to suffer the results of his passionate faithfulness to the radical message of God's unfailing love and mercy. Jesus' crucifixion exposed the fact that legitimate authority and law can be wrong.

Thérèse understood that God's justice is not like vengeful human justice. Jesus responded in a nonretaliating way to the horrific injustice that was done to him. His dying prayer, "Father, forgive them, they know not what they do" (Luke 23:34), expressed his compassionate forgiveness of the violence of the world. His undeserved crucifixion was redemptive: in this central Christian mystery of death and resurrection, God's love ensured that death would not have the last word over life.

Addressing the first corrosive assumption—that God is a cruel ruler requiring harsh punishment—Thérèse recognized that God's justice is enfolded within God's merciful love. With boldness and deep trust, she invited the sisters she lived with to accept the joy of letting go of the burden of fear. Thérèse knew in her heart that God's mercy and forgiveness would embrace their repentant hearts, no matter the depth of their wrongdoing and the weakness of their wills.

Human Justice

Thérèse observed a second damaging belief flowing from the first one. She saw that the distorted notion of God as exacting, vengeful, and unreasonably insistent on law and order had an impact on how people thought about human justice. It was a pattern in her culture that remains evident today. If God is seen as strict, legalistic, and punitive, then this validates the harshest aspects of our criminal justice systems.

On any given day, we can see reports in the news media about court cases in which the victims of violence insist on "justice." By this they mean a harsh prison sentence or even death, as if requiring a life for a life will make things right. If we think of God as a rule enforcer, then we can justify oppressive orders and capital punishment as "good violence."

While it is true that courageous action to protect the innocent from evil is sometimes necessary, forceful restraint does not equal hostile violence. We protect the innocent through the creative use of power that is animated by love, not by hatred.

In Thérèse's own life, she repeatedly demonstrated an unfailing confidence in the merciful God who would forgive those who had done wrong. Shortly after her complete conversion, she undertook prayer for a man named Henri Pranzini, a vicious murderer who had been condemned to death and for whom "everything pointed to the fact that he would die impenitent."[25] Thérèse never excused Pranzini's crimes, but she wanted "at all costs" to pray him into heaven and spare him from damnation.

Thérèse was absolutely confident that God would touch Pranzini's heart and pardon him, whether or not there were any public signs of his remorse. She resisted the cultural temptation toward feelings of revenge and stayed true to her confidence in God's limitless willingness to forgive. When the newspapers reported that Pranzini had asked to kiss a crucifix as he mounted the execution scaffold, Thérèse was moved to tears of joy.

Striving for Moral Excellence

Thérèse also helps us overcome a third damaging notion: the belief that we must achieve moral excellence on our own. When we hear a sermon telling us we must "strive" more in order to become good and worthy of God's approval, we are hearing rumblings of this false notion. Whether we try to get ourselves together because we think a critical God requires it or because society expects it, the risk is the same: we find ourselves thinking that we can and should make ourselves perfect or at least admirable.

The inherent violence of this idea is hard to notice because the belief is taken as a given. We get caught in the trap of thinking that it's up to us to get ourselves in shape—or else. This striving becomes a way of bullying ourselves, of being emotionally violent toward ourselves. One of the consequences of this mistaken belief is the tendency toward perfectionism, the belief that freedom from sin is attainable by our human efforts.

Thérèse, like many of us, was afflicted by her own form of perfectionism, evident in her childhood efforts to be good all the time. Although she experienced a powerful release from the grip of this compulsion at the moment of her complete conversion, she remained vulnerable to a perfectionist attitude. Yet her "treasure" was her awareness that she could trust God's love to enfold her, no matter how imperfect she was and would always be. She learned that in its essence, moral perfectionism runs counter to the idea that God is merciful, loving, and forgiving.

Thérèse noticed the negative effects of this striving to be perfect in the sincere people around her, especially the sisters she lived with and the priests whom she counseled through her letters. These good people were judgmental and critical, beating up on themselves and on one another as they strove to be holy and "good enough." Thérèse observed that if the sisters thought God was always sizing them up, if they couldn't trust that God was on their side, then they could hardly go to God for help when they found themselves in difficulty. It was up to them alone to become holy.

Thérèse was under no illusions that she had the capacity to become a great saint on her own. She knew she was in trouble if holiness depended on her effort. She had boundless confidence that God's love would do for her soul what she, by her own willfulness, could not do. Thérèse grasped with great clarity the fact that God is not vindictive, not cruel, not distant, not punitive. Even God's justice is clothed in mercy.

Mentoring Messages for Reflection

From her own experience of family love, Thérèse glimpsed the truth of God's immense love for us—even when, in our weakness, we fail to choose the good. As she put it, "One can never have too much confidence in God, who is so powerful and so merciful! One receives from Him quite as much as one hopes for!"[26]

Thérèse's confident vision reminds us of the gospel message that life flourishes when it is centered on love, not anxiety. Thérèse's conviction about the essential nonviolence and mercy of God points us to two powerful life lessons, one that frees our own hearts and another that frees those we are inclined to judge.

✧ God is on our side. We can be safe, healed, and freed, even though we are not perfect.

Each of us comes to the message of this chapter from a lifetime of imaging God in particular ways. We are influenced by our childhood experiences, our religious exposure, and our life journeys as adults. Some of us may already have banished the image of a punitive God and embraced the God of love, just as Thérèse did. Others may still carry vestiges of fear of God's judgment. Some may have turned away in anger, scandalized by cruel images of God. Far too many of us may carry the burden of believing we are responsible for shaping up and achieving virtue, fixing what's wrong with ourselves and with the world. We feel shame at our failures and wearied when our efforts seem fruitless.

Reflecting on Thérèse's transformational insight into the heart of a loving God can heal us. Such reflection can release us from unnecessary guilt and worry. Instead of imagining a wrathful God who refuses to acknowledge our inherent weakness and imperfection, we can look to the gospel revelation of God's essential mercy and loving nature. We are invited to exchange fear for safety, anxiety for trust.

✧ It isn't our job to enact "good violence" that punishes others, as if we are acting on God's behalf.

When we give in to judgmental attitudes, we unleash subtle violence.

Especially in polarized and stressful times, anger, fear, and bitterness can corrode the bonds of community. In place of compassion and patience, judgmental attitudes fly. We draw lines between "us" and "them," those we think are right and those we think are wrong. We can be caught in this irresistible emotional undertow.

Even deeper danger arises when we justify these battle lines by what we assume God wills or what we believe God accepts or rejects. The image of an unbending God or a rigid moral code takes over, and violent condemnations follow.

Thérèse's example shows us that we can see others, even opponents, with the eyes of God. That loving gaze and softened heart are miracles of love. Allowing God's love to move through us, we hope for the grace to suspend our judgmental thoughts and to see the humanity at the core of each person. This includes people we may consider to be "enemies."

Needless to say, we know how hard this can be. We repeatedly fail to meet the standard of compassionate, nonviolent respect for others. Again, we are human, not perfect. But what Dr. Martin Luther King, Jr., said is still true: "Darkness cannot drive out darkness; only light can do that. Hate cannot drive out hate; only love can do that."[27]

Chapter 4

What Is Love?
And Learning
What Love Is Not

A yearning for love is one of the most fundamental of human desires. Many of us are prone to romanticize the idea of love, as if it were something blissful and magical. But love in real life is complex, especially in our most intimate relationships, with family and friends.

In such close relationships, we are vulnerable. With our loved ones, we cherish the moments of affection and joy, but we also suffer the pain that our loved ones cause us, whether they intend to hurt us or not. And surely we love and hurt them in similar ways.

In this chapter, we will look at Thérèse's lifelong quest to understand love more clearly. She gained insight from reflecting on the words of St. Paul about what love *is* as well as what love *is not*. This chapter also examines more carefully the notion of violence and explores three ways in which Thérèse noticed that violence could creep into daily life.

What Is Love?

Thérèse's spirituality was grounded in the radical conviction that the God revealed by Jesus is like a forgiving and loving parent; even God's justice is clothed in mercy. Such an image came naturally to Thérèse, who grew up in a warm and loving family. Most of the time, however, she was immersed in a religious culture driven by fear of God's judgment and a relentless, impossible striving for perfection. In such circumstances, love was prone to distortion by shadows of subtle or even blatant violence.

Thérèse was largely on her own as she clung to her conviction of God's love as merciful and devoid of cruelty. With little support from the religious leaders whose teaching was available to her, Thérèse creatively searched for ways of loving action that would enable her to avoid violence to herself and others. She taught those under her guidance how to do the same, offering them reassurance and hope.

The writings of St. Paul especially helped Thérèse understand the nature of love. In one of the most quoted passages from the Scriptures, a favorite for wedding ceremonies, Paul said this:

> Love is patient, love is kind. It is not jealous, [love] is not pompous, it is not inflated, it is not rude, it does not seek its own interests, it is not quick-tempered, it does not brood over injury, it does not rejoice over wrongdoing but rejoices with the truth. It bears all things, believes all things, hopes all things, endures all things.
> Love never fails. (1 Corinthians 13:4-8)

This passage tells what love is, but Thérèse also paid attention to what love is *not*. It turns out that even St. Paul couldn't go much further in defining what love *is* besides saying that it is kind, patient, and enduring. It appeared easier for him to name all the ways people can be unloving than to describe the mystery of love.

With her practical focus, Thérèse recognized that St. Paul grounded his guidance in a savvy grasp of how people actually behave. Thérèse was looking for ways to be loving to real people in her real life. She wasn't chasing romantic or trivial ideas about love. Paul's words oriented her to the feelings and actions that reflect love as well as the ones that don't. She took seriously the importance of avoiding attitudes and behaviors that hold the seeds of violence.

St. Paul helped Thérèse see that if she was clear about the ways she did not want to be—rude, spiteful, arrogant, mean, self-centered, prickly, moody, or pompous—then she might be able to act in spontaneous and creative ways to be kind and loving. He confirmed for her that there isn't an *exact* prescription for how to be loving; she would have to discover it in the unpredictable circumstances of her life. What she could be sure of was that loving is kind, and it is patient; it is never violent to her own spirit or those of others.

Trusting in God's love for her, Thérèse did her best to cultivate patient love for others in her heart. This she did with simplicity, without making a fuss. From the outside, Thérèse's simple way may appear wimpish, but from the inside, her kindness was heroic.

In fact, it was impossible for Thérèse to be charitable and peaceful without sometimes getting stepped on. Loving is associated with necessary suffering. Thérèse experienced this suffering, she saw it in the life of Jesus, and she noticed, in the Gospels, how Jesus coped with it.

Thérèse saw that if Jesus did not comply with rules about religious behavior before preaching or acting charitably, people often criticized or threatened him. She saw how worn out he became with the constant press of people seeking healing and how he withdrew for times of prayer or solitude to replenish his spirit. At the last, when Jesus was violently executed, he maintained an attitude of love and forgiveness.

Like Jesus, Thérèse was not a pushover. She made prudent use of boundaries to protect herself from unkind violence. She used withdrawal as a psychological defense, including fleeing the scene if she needed to get a little space in order to hold her ground emotionally. "My *last means* of not being defeated in combats is desertion; I was already using this means during my novitiate, and it always succeeded perfectly with me."[28] As well as she could, she accepted the pain of loving without retaliating, in imitation of Jesus.

Hidden Violence

Love without violence is basic to the good, meaningful, and productive life that Thérèse offers us. But to take Thérèse's offer into our lives, we may have to expand our usual understanding of violence. Normally the word makes us think of brutal physical violations, such as murder, lynching, mass shootings, terrorism, rape, domestic abuse, war, and so on. "Violence" is a word usually applied to bloody, heartrending, and fearsome tragedies. If we witness it, we are left heartsick and traumatized.

But what about the more hidden violence of angry feelings, harsh thoughts, and cutting words, the malice that rises up *before* the blood flows? Blatant violence feeds on such shadowy violence. But this shadowy violence is also present in our lives apart from physical violence. And what about unintended violence, such as the personal violation we experience if we are innocently overlooked or thoughtlessly deprived of what is our due?

Violence in one form or another—blatant, shadowy, or unintended—entangles everyone. We don't need much help to notice the first type: the obvious shocking violence in human conflicts. Thérèse helps us see the more hidden forms of violence, which can be mixed in with acts of love.

Thérèse understood that we all suffer violence in our lives, some at the hands of people who intend the complete opposite. As a child, Thérèse was dearly loved but loved imperfectly. She experienced early separation from her family during her months with the wet nurse. The death of her mother and the departure of her sisters for the convent further destabilized her. It is possible that these early traumas led to feelings of not being sufficiently treasured; they wounded Thérèse's sense of security and safety. Surely they played a part in her tendency toward neediness and hypersensitivity. They led her to beat up on herself as she strove to meet her needs, a form of subtle violence against herself.

Thérèse arrived at an awareness of the connection between wounded hearts and subtle violence in daily life. With a sense of compassion for each person's vulnerabilities, she came to understand that everyday failures to love—the behaviors that St. Paul described as rude, spiteful, arrogant, mean, self-centered, prickly, moody, or pompous—happen often, and they injure us. In the convent, with two dozen other women, even holy women, Thérèse saw the burdens these hidden ways of violence placed on the community. A failure to be loving could appear in at least three ways: the everyday violence inflicted on us by others, the hidden violence we impose on others, and the shadowy violence we pass on to ourselves. We may be most accustomed to noticing the first failure: the violence others inflict on us. We experience this when an insecure bully pushes us around; when insulting words come our way; when racism, sexism, or some other intolerance inflicts its pain; or when hostile silence greets us. We may not be used to calling such things violence, but we definitely feel the sting of even casual or unconscious disrespect.

The second failure to love is violence we impose on others. Perhaps we steamroll others to get our way, we seek revenge for a perceived slight, or we react with passive aggression to someone who irritates us. Cutting remarks, the unfunny joke at another's expense, contemptuous mockery of political opponents or people who are different are all forms of daily human violence. It's a form of unloving violence when we give someone the silent treatment or when we shun those whose life choices we judge to be wrong.

Despite our best intentions, we fall into such behaviors with distressing frequency. It may bring us up short to think that our snarky, mean, or piously self-righteous behavior is violent, but it is. If it is accepted as normal, such casual disrespect feeds a culture of hate from which more lethal violence can eventually erupt.

Finally, the third unloving behavior, one that almost always goes unnoticed, is to inflict violence on ourselves. Perhaps we subject ourselves to what psychologists have named "the tyranny of the shoulds," leading to self-induced guilt trips. Or we go along with a group opinion or decision that we don't think is right. We are violent toward ourselves if we regularly override our genuine needs because we want to retain the approval of another.

Thomas Merton spoke of this pattern when addressing activists for peace: "To allow oneself to be carried away by a multitude of conflicting concerns, to surrender to too many demands, to commit oneself to too many projects, to want to help everyone in everything is to succumb to violence."[29]

These examples of emotional violence often are hidden within the appearance of normal life. Without defensiveness or denial, Thérèse saw that a tendency to this kind of violence is real for all of us—people who are far from likely to literally kill anyone. Most important, Thérèse saw that a truly loving life would have to avoid any form of coercive bullying.

Nonviolence: The Essence of Love

For many people, the word "nonviolence" sounds more sterile than "violence." It tends to have political overtones. It makes us think of Gandhi or the Rev. Dr. Martin Luther King, Jr. We may associate nonviolence with civil disobedience and protest marches, forms of peaceful resistance to oppression.

For Thérèse, nonviolence was the essence of love. The practical, actionable words of St. Paul illuminated the overflowing, generous, merciful love of God, to which Thérèse entrusted her heart and her life. When we reach out to another with love, we participate in the very character of God, in our limited and imperfect way. If it is true that we are made in the image and likeness of God, then love is like a default setting for our hearts.

It is true that, faced with a threat, love requires us to set realistic boundaries. We must constrain those who intend to do harm. We can set limits respectfully, without hostility but with firmness. We'll look more closely at the challenge of boundary setting in chapter eight, which addresses the heart quality of compassion.

Mentoring Messages for Reflection

The takeaways from Thérèse's insights into love are, thankfully, very much within our grasp. If we pay attention, we will find that we, like Thérèse, can express love without violence in our daily life—in small ordinary gestures. And when we fail, as we inevitably will, nonviolence encourages us to forgive our imperfect selves.

✧ If we remind ourselves of anything each day, it might be this: "Love is patient, love is kind" (1 Corinthians 13:4).

Popular ideas of love are like fairy tales, leading us to imagine that if we love someone, then acting toward them in a loving way will be effortless. But in the real world, acting in a loving way takes intention and self-discipline. More specifically, it takes patience and kindness.

In daily life, tired children can be cranky, elders can wear us out with their repetitive worries, and overworked spouses can forget to do the errand they promised. Remembering in the nick of time to take a breath and extend our patience after a stressful day at home, we may manage to eke out a bit more tolerance and a genuinely kind word or smile, even if we are perilously close to the frayed end of our patience. Loving warmth softens the tension in us and in others. It makes possible a way through the stress, without meanness.

At work our love might involve putting aside resentment or retaliation and maintaining instead an even-tempered attitude toward uncooperative colleagues. We can try to understand work situations more deeply before we jump to negative conclusions: sometimes the true dimensions of an issue can become clear only if we resist the instinct to blame others.

In all these examples, the loving way is making a choice to think and act kindly, to extend our patience, to do our best to respond to the other the way we would hope someone would respond to us. Even when we take assertive actions like setting boundaries, correcting a child, or speaking up for what we rightly can expect from another person, we can try to speak from a position of kindness, without the hard edge of indignation or anger. In a reflective spirit, we might consider what part we have played in the situations that test our patience. We can then adjust our expectations of others and of ourselves in realistic ways.

✧ When we inevitably stumble in our intentions to love without violence, pushing ourselves harder is just more violence.

We are only human; we aren't going to be perfect at this. Making the loving choice can be difficult. It's a great temptation to nurse our anger, contempt, or self-righteousness, especially toward those we think deserve it.

The sensitive and self-aware Thérèse was no different from us as she tried to be more loving. Once she grasped this vision of love without violence, she realized that she would also have to acknowledge her inability to be successful, on her own, at loving. In seeing her weaknesses, Thérèse recognized that she could not simply push herself harder; after all, that stance of strenuous effort and self-achievement would itself be a violent approach to her own limitations and weaknesses.

Thérèse, our mentor, offers us the profound insight that love without violence means mercy and forgiveness toward ourselves as well as others when—inevitably—we haven't been able to completely avoid violence or prevent harm. Practicing self-compassion, we forgive ourselves for failing and resolve with a willing heart to do better the next time.

Thérèse didn't reproach herself for her failures; instead, she felt immense gratitude for God's merciful love. Her vision of the infinitely loving God opened her heart.

Chapter 5

Healing from Perfectionism

Many people have a tendency toward perfectionism. In minor matters, perfectionism might be mildly annoying but not a big deal. It becomes more serious when it pushes and bullies us on the inside and when we transfer that demanding pressure onto those around us.

Sometimes it feels as if we can't escape the critical voice of the stern internal overseer that keeps wanting us to do more and do better. Perfectionism is a grim and exhausting way to go through life. Healing from it is one of the most liberating gifts of Thérèse's wisdom.

Perfectionism played a role in Thérèse's spirit until her complete conversion. Even after that transforming event, she had to manage the temptation to be a perfectionist. It was precisely her sincere but unsuccessful efforts to achieve holiness on her own that led her to the discovery that she called her "Little Way," her distinctive understanding of spiritual and emotional maturity. In her willingness to walk in trust, free

of fear, Thérèse found relief from the harsh and useless effort
that marks perfectionism.

The Subtle Violence of Perfectionism

Thérèse's perfectionist tendencies began as they do for most
people: as responses to the wounds of her early life. In her
childhood, especially after her mother's death, she became
overly intent on pleasing her father and older sisters. Mistaken religious messages of the time further compounded
that tendency: sermons, for example, that urged the elim-
ination of inadequacies and sins through one's own effort.
This interpretation of perfection trapped Thérèse in a
cycle of effort, disappointment, and more effort. Trying
to become perfect was for her a recipe for psychological
and spiritual violence.

Even as a child, Thérèse applied her formidable willpower
to her self-improvement. She tried hard to stay on everyone's
good side—including God's, to spare God some suffering. But
her efforts didn't go well; she eventually realized she was getting nowhere.

Thérèse tells us of her erratic behavior during that time
in this poignant passage, gently leavened with her wry sense
of humor:

> If I happened to cause anyone I loved some little trouble,
> even unwittingly, instead of forgetting about it and not
> *crying*, which made matters worse, I *cried* like a Magda-
> lene and then when I began to cheer up, I'd begin to *cry*

again for having cried. . . . I was quite unable to correct this terrible fault.[30]

Thérèse knew that striving to be perfect was hopeless and joyless. Recognizing that she was into a "terrible fault," she gained insight into the violence that such self-improvement represented for her. She began to understand that striving for perfection was often a form of psychological and spiritual self-defense. Perfectionism could be a self-centered way to make sure that others would be impressed and remain close to her. Thus it damaged her sense of integrity.

In the watershed moment of her complete conversion, Thérèse began to see that she could bear the feelings of being imperfect. She could trust that her real self would be good enough and that God would supply what she lacked.

Discovery of a "Little Way"

Even into her convent years, Thérèse remained sensitive to the temptation to push, to strive, to make herself better. The cloister was a place to achieve perfection, according to the religious messages Thérèse heard. The holiness of the religious life was an accomplishment beyond ordinary people. At the Carmelite convent, preaching in conferences and retreats used images like ascending the arduous stairway of perfection, mastering the laborious stages of virtue, and climbing the rugged heights of self-inflicted penances.

The call was daunting for Thérèse, who had applied herself for years to imitating the saints. Despite her effort and goodwill, Thérèse acknowledged that she couldn't see herself achieving the significant accomplishments of "big" souls. She had always seen herself as a "little" soul, trusting that God would not abandon her.

Then, during an unusual convent retreat, Thérèse made a decisive, liberating advance. She came to understand that even though she might continue to be disappointed in herself, her failures didn't offend God or cause God pain. She felt herself launched "full sail upon the waves of *confidence and love*," consoled because "never had I heard that our faults *could not cause God any pain*, and this assurance filled me with joy."[31]

In this newfound hope, Thérèse wrote these significant words: "I want to seek out a means of going to heaven by a little way, a way that is very straight, very short, and totally new."[32] Inspired by imagination and desire, Thérèse would find what she was looking for.

Instead of struggling up the rough mountain of holiness with its emphasis on self-denial or climbing the stairway of perfection with its many steps, Thérèse considered the image of an elevator, a new invention that she encountered as a teenager on a trip to Rome. If only there were an elevator in the spiritual life that could raise her up, replacing the rough mountains and long stairways and steep ladders that would lead to perfect virtue. She knew immediately that the spiritual life did have such an elevator! "The elevator which must raise me to heaven is Your arms, O Jesus! And for this I had no need to grow up, but rather I had to remain *little*."[33]

Just as her mother had lifted her as a child up the stairs, which were too much for her little legs, Thérèse's loving God was ready to stoop down, lift her up, and transform her. She didn't need to struggle and climb, to be other than her imperfect self. God would do the heavy lifting; it was that simple.

With the image of the elevator, Thérèse captured a profound insight into the fundamental message of the gospel. She didn't have to save herself; she couldn't anyway. The transcendent love that enfolds us—the mystery of God—saves us. It was sufficient that she bring her willingness to love God, trust God, and do her best to live a life of love.

Thérèse's simple honesty, in acknowledging that she couldn't achieve sanctity with her own efforts, was precisely what prompted her to look for the "elevator" of God's love. Rejoicing at this revelation, she felt released from the stern pressure of the prevailing religious mentality. Her heart registered that this Little Way of trust in the love of God was more faithful to the gospel than the narrative of willful striving that surrounded her.

Redefining Perfection

In embracing this truth, Thérèse felt release from the violence of perfectionism. She drew strength and confidence from her realization that working on making herself perfect was neither possible nor necessary. As she matured, she avoided bullying herself as much as she could. When she failed to curb her striving efforts to do good or to be pleasing, she accepted the feelings that came with failure, deepening her humble relationship with an accepting God, and continued on.

In the spirit of St. Paul, she wrote of her willingness to "bear with myself such as I am with all my imperfections"[34] "I am not disturbed at seeing myself weakness itself. On the contrary, it is in my weakness that I glory, and I expect each day to discover new imperfections in myself."[35]

As she meditated on Jesus' parables in the Scriptures, Thérèse identified with the publican who drew God's mercy when he relinquished his bragging rights and acknowledged his imperfections. True to the deeper message of the gospel, she wrote, "Perfection consists in doing His will, in being what He wills us to be."[36] She invited herself and those she guided to embrace this truth, no matter how much they might wish to be someone "better" or "perfect." Later in her life, she wrote, "[P]erfection seems simple to me, I see it is sufficient to recognize one's nothingness and to abandon oneself as a child into God's arms."[37]

In an especially revealing comment, Thérèse briefly and powerfully describes her youthful belief that holiness meant perfection, then her mature awareness that this was not true:

> At the beginning of my spiritual life when I was thirteen or fourteen, I used to ask myself what I would have to strive for later on because I believed it was quite impossible for me to understand perfection better. I learned very quickly since then that the more one advances, the more one sees the goal is still far off. And now I am simply resigned to see myself always imperfect and in this I find my joy.[38]

Teaching Céline the Little Way

Over time Thérèse was increasingly confident of her grasp of authentic gospel spirituality, her Little Way. Using the language of littleness to represent humble honesty, Thérèse encouraged her sisters in the convent to bear with their inadequacies: "YES, it suffices to humble oneself, to bear with one's imperfections. That is real sanctity!"[39] She made this truth—that God's power is the source of holiness—the basis for her guidance of the young novices and in particular her sister Céline.

Céline was Thérèse's soul mate and most intimate confidante during their childhood. As the four other Martin sisters, including Thérèse, entered convents, Céline remained at home to care for their father. After he died, she joined the Carmelite community at Lisieux. Céline, the novice nun, now found herself under the tutelage of the younger Thérèse, who had left home eight years earlier. Although Thérèse was one of the youngest Carmelites, she was such a respected member of the community that the superior asked her to assist with the spiritual formation of the new members.

From their shared childhood, Thérèse had a good sense of Céline's nature and of her determined, willful spirit. After all, Thérèse had moved away from this attitude in herself as she grew up. Now she tried to help her sister understand the falsity in her frustrated attempts to be a good religious.

Céline was confronting the contrast between her romantic vision of a holy life in the convent and the mundane reality of congregate life—just as Thérèse had during her own novitiate.

Céline often felt embarrassed and disappointed by her weaknesses and irritated by the moments of friction with difficult sisters. Seeking a sympathetic ear perhaps, she brought her complaints to Thérèse. Céline found fault with herself and lamented to Thérèse that she "had so much *to acquire*" in order to become a good religious sister.[40]

Thérèse recognized that Céline was reacting to her imperfections in a spirit of striving and willfulness, condemning herself and doing violence to herself. She responded to Céline's lament with a brief phrase that encapsulated the wisdom of the Little Way: "Rather," she said, "how much you have *to lose*."[41]

Thérèse meant that if Céline were to come to God by the Little Way, it would not involve self-condemnation for imperfections and willful efforts for self-improvement. She was inviting Céline to drop her entanglements with her hidden self-centered agenda and recognize her weaknesses in a spirit of self-surrender, humility, and trust in God's love for her.

Some months after that exchange, a despondent Céline again reproached herself in a note to Thérèse. Céline was distressed because she felt inadequate in preparing to receive the Holy Child into her heart at Christmas. Thérèse encouraged her sister: "If you are able to bear serenely the trial of being displeasing to yourself, then you will be for Jesus a pleasant place of shelter."[42] Thérèse was assuring Céline that Jesus would find a place of shelter in an honest heart, not a perfect heart.

In the phrase "to bear serenely the trial of being displeasing to yourself," Thérèse packs a lot of wisdom. She leads Céline away from a frustrated, self-blaming, self-violent reaction. She encourages her sister to make peace with her messy reality, humbly accepting the truth with kindness, not animosity, and entering the elevator of God's arms.

The word "serenely" is important here. Céline might have grudgingly tried to bear her disappointment; bearing it serenely goes beyond simple tolerance to a truly peaceful heart. Over and over, Thérèse gently invited Céline and others to the two essential steps on the path of the Little Way, her only treasure: honestly accepting their true selves and welcoming God's love into their grateful hearts.

The Little Way: Not Passive, Not Painless

Thérèse confidently shared the reassuring message of her Little Way with those she counseled. As she didn't scold herself when she failed, she didn't suggest to those she guided that they reproach or punish themselves. She advised them to acknowledge their mistakes honestly and compassionately and to implore God's mercy while continuing to do their best to be loving. She helped them avoid becoming adversaries to themselves, to others, or to the circumstances of life.

Thérèse knew that her Little Way could sound deceptively simple. When one of the sisters spoke of wanting to share what she was learning with her parents, Thérèse advised caution. She was aware that, if badly explained, her Little Way could be misconstrued as passive and easy, almost like a spiritual get-out-of-jail-free card. But her way of love was not passive; it was not based on indifference, immaturity, or irresponsibility.

Thérèse wasn't teaching that the spiritual life makes no demands. In fact, she warned the sisters that following the path of love has inescapable moments of suffering; it is not a life for the self-indulgent. She passionately encouraged them to embrace the truth and accept the love of God that came to them freely, unearned. She showed them that the authentic response to such love is a life of kindness, service, and justice, lived with gratitude and a peaceful heart.

There was a paradox at work here for Thérèse: her understanding of herself not only enabled her to honestly accept her weaknesses but also freed her to act boldly and confidently from her genuine strengths, without getting tangled up in self-centeredness. Her trust that she was held in love energized her; it animated her willingness to put her gifts toward the service of the good. As a result, especially toward the end of her life, she exuded serenity and grace, creativity and compassion, and a spirit of gratefulness—qualities that attracted others to her.

Yet with all Thérèse's teaching and example, her Little Way still seemed too passive to her older sister Pauline. Like Céline, Pauline also had to mature in God's way. Only years after Thérèse's death did Pauline come to describe the Little Way more accurately: "Sanctity does not consist of this or that practice; it consists in a disposition of heart which makes us humble and little in the arms of God, conscious of our weakness, and confident to the point of audacity in the goodness of our Father."[43]

Thérèse was secure in her trust that this Little Way of non-violent love was God's way. Thus she invites us to forgive ourselves and to welcome his love and pardon, with trust that we are loved in spite of our flaws.

Mentoring Messages for Reflection

The Little Way reflects a deep-down realization that the path to a good life is not through our personal accomplishments; rather, it's though an embrace of the truth that we are loved as we are. The perspective of the Little Way can unchain us from the oppressive weight of our own perfectionism.

✧ If we want to let go of our perfectionism, we may have to grieve a loss: the dream of our perfect self.

The embarrassment of not living up to what we imagine we "should be" can lead to violence toward ourselves. Dwelling on our mistakes and failures, we beat ourselves up. The perfectionist in us is a stern judge. Preoccupied with the knowledge that we are flawed, we can devalue the truth that we are also good.

It may take many years, great suffering, sensitive therapy, or spiritual direction before we are ready to let go of the compulsion of perfectionism. It is present in us for a reason. In its own distorted way, perfectionism defends us from facing our unavoidable limitations by occupying us with an impossible ideal. If we want to let go of our perfectionism, we may need to grieve the loss of the perfect self that we imagine we could be through our own efforts.

Coming to embrace our own true self as loved by God is not unlike the process of learning to love and be loved by a marriage partner or our vowed community as a real and imperfect person, after the rose-colored glasses are set aside. Only as we are confident of being truly loved as we are—rough edges included—can we be free to grow into the best version of ourselves. Thérèse reminds us that we are called to accept the reality that we are only human and to believe the good news that we are loved *as* only human.

Thérèse's advice "to bear serenely the trial of being displeasing to yourself" is simple and profound mentoring. It's a healing message for those of us prone to feeling inadequate or guilty whenever we fall short of our own or someone else's expectations. However, it really is a big "ask" of our determined self.

Thérèse is not suggesting that we blithely ignore the times when we may have injured another or truly messed something up. Our feelings of regret—for displeasing ourselves—signal our recognition of the harm we may have caused and our sorrow about it. What we can take from Thérèse is the willingness to learn from our failure and to bear it without self-scolding.

Thérèse invites us to kindly say, "You're doing your best. Forgive yourself for not being able to be, or do, all that you desire. You are loved even though you aren't perfect. Let go of the upset feeling, and bring a peaceful heart to God and to the others with whom you share your life."

In releasing our tight grip on the idea that we must be perfect, we may find that our life is more authentic and fulfilling.

✧ The determined pursuit of perfection comes at a high price. We may gain peace when we notice what truly brings us joy.

We can look forward to joy and relief as we lay down the burden of perfectionism. But the journey to self-acceptance faces strong headwinds in our contemporary society. We are surrounded by a culture in which the compulsion to be perfect can be toxic and stressful, inhibiting authentic and meaningful life. Our mail and news feeds overflow with books, websites, and celebrities sending us the impossible message that we can and should get it together through our own determined efforts.

The supposed power of self-improvement can become an idol. Many of us feel intense pressure to live up to the expectations of our families, our communities, and our workplaces. It feels as if the stress doesn't let up, especially if we carry leadership responsibilities. We can feel trapped.

Thérèse might invite us to notice the inner violence we suffer as we wrestle ourselves into heroes at work or at home. Honest reflection on our strivings might give us a glimpse of the needs that we are trying to meet with such relentless effort. We may see that some of our achievements have come at the price of increasing anxiety, depression, or exhaustion. Life on our own particular treadmill could be costing us our health, our relationships, or our true self.

Thérèse might further ask us to reflect on what brings us joy, meaning, satisfaction. What could be healing for us? Such questions make the perfectionist in us feel vaguely guilty; they seem self-indulgent. And yet, with her characteristically gentle straight talk, Thérèse might suggest that these life-giving feelings come from a deep source within us: God's presence. The things that bring us authentic joy and inner peace are guideposts on the path of love.

Seriously reflecting on our joys and sufferings in a spirit of acceptance and gratitude leads us to grow into healthier patterns of living. Moving toward healing is an individual path, an internal process. If we decide to make changes in our behavior, it is also an external process. As we heal, we are better able to care for others.

✧ Self-knowledge and self-acceptance help us
be more effective coaches, managers, parents,
mentors, or teachers.

Thérèse points to the power of self-knowledge and self-acceptance as well as the value of managing our impulsive feelings. The answer to feeling trapped is not just in the outside world. If we change jobs or relationships or if we blame others—without facing our own demanding internal taskmaster—we will get to the same stuck place again.

When asked how to live a meaningful and good life, one sage simply said, "Tell the truth." Being honest with ourselves is a good place to begin. Bearing our dismay when we face our limitations will sting at first, and perhaps it will never get easy. But with practice, we can gain the confidence that, even though we *will* disappoint ourselves and others, we can take a deep breath and be willing to forgive and love our imperfect self as much as God does.

What's more, realizing that we are *all* imperfect moves us to nonviolent love for others. A perfectionist supervisor can be a terror for subordinates, but managers who have survived mistakes and inadequacy have the potential to be trusted coaches for those still learning the ropes. The same goes for parents and teachers.

Some may worry that avoiding perfectionism would mean settling for work results that are not up to snuff. That's not how Thérèse saw it. In fact, we ought to do our best to perform our duties, especially if we have responsibilities on which others depend. (That's certainly the attitude that we hope for from airline pilots and surgeons, for example.)

What Thérèse recognized as impossible is the ideal that we never make a mistake. She would urge us to just do our best, to be conscientious and thankful when things go well and patient when they don't.

Chapter 6

A Life Worth Living

We may find ourselves attracted to the idea of living a reflective life; it promises more grounded and peaceful days. It is intriguing to think that this ordinary human process of reflection was the primary method by which Thérèse moved forward in her psychological and spiritual development. She relied on nothing fancy—no tablets on a mountaintop or miraculous visions—just patient attention to the inner life.

In that very simplicity lies one of the biggest challenges for busy people today. Our modern world makes it hard to carve out reflective space. Even if we find ourselves more often at home or isolated from others, our technology severely undermines the potential for the rhythms of a reflective life. Yet for our physical, emotional, and spiritual health, we need to listen to our lives.

In Thérèse's case, her wisdom and maturity grew gradually, daily, out of her lifelong practice of reflecting honestly on her experience, whether life brought her joy or pain. We might call this habit of hers "thinking things over" or "mindfulness" or "getting in touch with her heart." It was a practice that Thérèse called prayer.

Thérèse knew that prayer isn't a matter of mimicking behaviors and external practices; rather, it arises from within. Prayer arose within her restless heart as she searched for peace, connectedness, love, and truth.

Prayer and Spirit Entwined

We know that Thérèse was perceptive and reflective from a very young age. Hers was a devout family who said prayers together regularly. Thérèse also developed a way of privately musing about life, nature, and mystery. She writes lightheartedly that sometimes she would lie in bed in the morning, "for it was there I made my profound meditations."[44] Sometimes Thérèse would steal away to the garden to reflect on her life. There she delighted in flowers in the daytime and starlight at night.

The powerful natural forces of lightning and thunder excited Thérèse, as did the wide expanses of the sky and the endless ocean. She saw her life and all of nature as the works of the generous Creator. When the child Thérèse went on fishing excursions with her father, "Sometimes I would try to fish with my little line, but I preferred to go *alone* and sit down on the grass bedecked with flowers, and then my thoughts became very profound indeed!"[45]

Thérèse wrote about these childhood habits from her vantage point as a Carmelite: "I understand now that I was making mental prayer without knowing it."[46] In the convent, Thérèse faithfully participated in formal times of prayer, but the spirit of reflective prayer that characterized her personal way was like the air she breathed.

Thérèse didn't have a formal name for this habit of reflection. She wrote:

> One day, one of my teachers at the Abbey asked me what I did on my free afternoons when I was alone. I told her I went behind my bed in an empty space which was there, and that it was easy to close myself in with my bed curtain and that "I *thought*." "But what do you think about?" she asked. "I think about God, about life, about *ETERNITY. . . . I think!*" The good religious laughed heartily at me, and later on she loved reminding me of the time when I *thought*, asking me if *I was still thinking.*[47]

Prayer Is Given to Us

As Thérèse understood it, a reflective, prayerful spirit is an intuitive orientation of the heart; it is something given to us. In his Epistle to the Romans, St. Paul says that we don't know how to pray as we ought but that the Spirit moves within us, searching our hearts, empowering and focusing us, bringing peace to our restlessness (see 8:26-27). Our desire for authenticity fosters our prayer, allowing the Spirit of God to pray in us.

Thérèse noticed that Jesus often took time apart from others. His regular practice of solitude and reflection nurtured a pervading awareness of and trust in God's providence; he constantly welcomed his Father's will.

Even though she had been exposed to many ideas about how holy people pray and even though she meditated on Jesus' own prayer, Thérèse understood that she was intuitively led to God in her unique yet ordinary human concerns. Prayer, she understood, is not something someone has to teach us, and it doesn't happen only at specific times and places or with specific formulas. She wasn't intimidated by any notion that she must pray the way she imagined saints or spiritual teachers prayed.

Thérèse confidently trusted that God was with her as she navigated the everyday ups and downs in her life as a religious sister. She wrote,

> Jesus has no need of books or teachers to instruct souls. . . . Never have I heard Him speak, but I feel that He is within me at each moment; He is guiding and inspiring me with what I must say and do. I find just when I need them certain lights that I had not seen until then, and it isn't most frequently during my hours of prayer that these are most abundant but rather in the midst of my daily occupations.[48]

With her typical refreshing candor, Thérèse gently set aside the supposed superiority of beautifully written prayers in favor of the simplicity of her thoughts and feelings. Her reflective attention to the ordinary moments of her life was her way of being receptive to God's presence. She knew that it is from within our hearts that the spirit of prayer moves. Eloquent or insightful thoughts are not necessary. In fact, Thérèse confided,

> I do not have the courage to force myself to search out *beautiful* prayers in books. There are so many of them it really

gives me a headache! and each prayer is more *beautiful* than the others. I cannot recite them all and not knowing which to choose, I do like children who do not know how to read, I say very simply to God what I wish to say, without composing beautiful sentences, and He always understands me.[49]

Thérèse grasped the fact that prayer is not about efforts to change what God thinks or to dictate what God will do. It is about coming to a deeper relationship with God so that we can receive God's love. Prayer changes *us*, not God. It allows us to see how we might be more loving persons; it challenges us to become more the image and likeness of God.

In her relationship with God, Thérèse didn't live in her head, in the realm of theories, but in heartfelt intimacy. In her role as counselor of new members of the community, she often recommended that it would be better to talk *to* God than to talk *about* God. Never did Thérèse live three inches off the ground amid ecstasies and visions.

And she certainly didn't flaunt her superiority. She readily admitted that, even in her prayer, she was weak and filled with tendencies toward vanity and self-centeredness. The knowledge of her own weaknesses called her to abandon herself to God's will.

Flowing from Thérèse's confidence in God's ever-present love, a prayerful spirit infused her actions and reflections, even if she wasn't praying in a formal way with the community or privately in her room or in the chapel. In fact, Thérèse candidly acknowledged how often she fell asleep during times of communal prayer and even during her private prayer:

> I should be desolate for having slept (for seven years) during
> my hours of prayer and my *thanksgivings* after Holy Commu-
> nion; well, I am not desolate. I remember that *little children*
> are as pleasing to their parents when they are asleep as well
> as when they are wide awake.[50]

She remained confident that her natural habit of reflection
kept her open to God's presence.

Thérèse's story shows us that she was by nature a reflective,
even contemplative, child. Her insights matured gradually. She
remained confident that she could communicate with God in
her own unique way and that this would be fine. At the end
of her life, having always welcomed intimacy with Jesus, who
identified himself as the Truth, she said to the sisters, "Y*es, it
seems I never looked for anything but the truth.*"[51]

Thérèse's Description of Prayer

With natural authority, Thérèse teaches us how to pray.
She wrote a description of prayer that now appears in the
Catechism of the Catholic Church as the first answer to the
question "What is prayer?"

> For me, prayer is a surge of the heart; it is a simple look
> turned toward heaven, it is a cry of recognition and of love,
> embracing both trial and joy. (*Catechism*, 2558, quoting
> *Manuscrits autobiographiques*, C 25r)

Perhaps the first thing we notice about this description of
prayer is that Thérèse begins with the words "for me." Her

phrasing is a gentle, invitational way to share her experiences with others, not to dictate how prayer should be for anyone else. Her words respect the deeply personal nature of the Spirit's movement in each of us. She frees us to pray the way we *can* without worrying about praying the way we *can't*.

Thérèse touches on three forms of prayer that many spiritual traditions have recognized. By speaking of a "surge of the heart," she describes prayer as something that emerges from the intuition of our hearts and moves our feelings. Prayer is the sense of welcoming wholeheartedly the presence of mystery that transcends us.

When Thérèse calls prayer "a simple glance turned toward heaven," she affirms that prayer flows in silence as we focus on the presence of mystery. This singular focus lives in us as a spirit of faith, as trust and confidence.

And finally, in using the words "embracing both trial and joy," Thérèse validates the way that ordinary people like us have always prayed. We reflect on the sadness and joys of our lives; that is, we pray our experiences, turning things over in our minds as we search for the meaning of our lives.

We Touch the Loving Heart of God

Envisioning God as an infinitely loving father, Thérèse was most at home with the imagery of God's arms reaching out to embrace us. One priest who wrote to Thérèse for spiritual direction said that when he prayed for forgiveness, he prayed "at the feet of God." "I beg you," Thérèse wrote back, "do not *drag* yourself any longer to *His feet*; follow that 'first impulse that draws you into His arms.'"[52]

In another letter to this priest, Thérèse included a parable of two mischievous children and their father, who is always prepared to pardon the son who takes him "by his heart":

> I would like to try to make you understand by means of a very simple comparison how much Jesus loves even imperfect souls who confide in Him:
>
> I picture a father who has two children, mischievous and disobedient, and when he comes to punish them, he sees one of them who trembles and gets away from him in terror, having, however, in the bottom of his heart the feeling that he deserves to be punished; and his brother, on the contrary, throws himself into his father's arms, saying that he is sorry for having caused him any trouble, that he loves him, and to prove it he will be good from now on, and if this child asks his father to *punish* him with a *kiss*, I do not believe that the heart of the happy father could resist the filial confidence of his child, whose sincerity and love he knows.
>
> He realizes, however, that more than once his son will fall into the same faults, but he is prepared to pardon him always, if his son always takes him by his heart.[53]

The story is vintage Thérèse, showing us the warmth and intimacy with which she prayed. The father's feelings about the disobedient behavior are not punitive; he wasn't keeping score. Thérèse knew that God responds to us with the same compassionate willingness to be present to us. She had absolute confidence that God will always forgive the child who returns with repentance and love.

Our personal images of God may be different from Thérèse's vision of a compassionate Father. We may be more drawn to the feminine and motherly features of a loving parent, or we may resonate with images of the Creator, Spirit of Wisdom, or Divine Friend. As we mature in life, our images of God evolve as well; God meets us where we are. What we take from Thérèse is a reminder of what will never change: the merciful and forgiving love in which God securely holds us.

Mentoring Messages for Reflection

Thérèse grew in wisdom through her habit of reflecting on her life experiences. As she thought about the events of her day, facing her feelings, she placed her life in God's hands. If insight and peace came, she was grateful. If distress and frustration remained, she was patient with herself. We can follow her lead, as she mentors us into a reflective life.

✧ Taking time to listen to our lives is basic to our emotional health.

The practice of attentive reflection that was so important to Thérèse's maturation isn't intrinsically difficult; it might even seem easy to imitate. But reflective space is vanishing these days, as we are consumed by phones, tablets, laptops, and the permanent connectivity they provide. Now the cup of coffee or the bus ride or the wait in line at the store involves checking for texts from the family, reviewing emails from work, and keeping an eye on the latest news feed. For many of us, this has become an addictive behavior, a challenge we need to recognize.

Our hopes, worries, and dreams percolate inside and come up in their own time. If we suppress them for too long, they can show up as physical symptoms of stress. The ability to reflect on our experiences is fundamental for our emotional health. Without such reflection, we become frazzled, anxious, and splintered in our attention. The push and pull of daily living wear us out—perhaps driving us to addictions and compulsions, to escapist screen time, to comfort food, and to willful efforts that bully others and ourselves.

Becoming more reflective means learning how to listen to our inner self no matter how messy our reality is. It means honestly noticing our actual feelings and desires, with compassion for ourselves and those with whom we live and work. Reviewing our lives this way, open to the loving providence of the Divine, is a way of praying and perhaps the most natural one for most of us. It is also something we might overlook and not even regard as prayer.

What's important is that we do not fill all our time with "stuff" to do. If that happens, there's little room for the inner process. When we feel that we are losing ourselves, we have to stop something. It's not so much about what *to do* as about what *not to do*.

✧ There are many small daily ways to touch on reflection. We each find our unique way of praying.

If we'd like to change our habits of distraction, it may be most realistic to begin with small opportunities to build a reflective spirit. In fact, we'll probably be better off with a simple practice, something that isn't too hard. Perfectionism is likely to run amok if we set about trying to "do the reflection thing right." We can begin by taking five or ten minutes on a regular basis to attend to how we feel and what we need.

In the morning, we might set aside moments to reflect on what the day holds, including occasions when we might need to be patient, to listen, to forgive, to take a time-out. Or we might take a few moments at night to quietly reflect on the day. Sharing our experiences with others—through conversations with a close friend, a spiritual director, or a prayer group—is another way to prayerfully review our lives. This kind of sharing can also happen through letter writing, as was common in Thérèse's lifetime.

Journal writing—sometimes in the form of a dialogue with God—meditation, and prayerful walks outdoors, in which we can recognize our smallness in the vastness of creation, can build a reflective spirit within us. A reflective moment might even arrive during ordinary tasks, like pulling weeds, folding laundry, or enjoying art or music. If the very notion of a quiet minute seems impossible to the parents of small children, God can be trusted to hold us in love until we have the chance to breathe again. What's important is that we silence the chatter of the world around us, even temporarily, so that we can be present to the stirrings of our hearts.

Thérèse is proof that our personal way of developing a reflective life is authentic and good. We need not try to pray the way we imagine we ought to pray—like a monk, a meditation master, or a mystic. We can trust that we will intuitively be led to what Thérèse understood to be the universal spirit of reflective prayer.

Part II

Six Heart
Qualities
of
Thérèse's
Healing Vision

Thérèse could express the core of her Little Way, her "only treasure," succinctly in two essential steps: honestly accepting our imperfect selves and trustfully welcoming God's love for us and for everyone. Hers was a way of living, not a set of theological ideas to study. Each day she did her best to receive love and to share love in the circumstances of her life, whether she was at home with her family or in the convent with her religious sisters.

So how did Thérèse know when her ordinary daily actions were taking her on this Little Way, the path of a loving life without violence to herself or others? In the whirl of activities and feelings, what attitudes and behaviors signaled that she was heading in the right direction?

As we study Thérèse's writings, we are able to discern six heart qualities that indicated she was on the right path:

- inner freedom
- compassion
- creativity
- a willing spirit
- gratefulness
- self-surrender

These qualities are the psychological and spiritual attitudes that Thérèse cultivated and that she mentors in us.

In Part II we will explore these six heart qualities. Although we are going to consider each one separately, they are interconnected in spirit and practice, each one contributing to the whole of a loving life.

Chapter 7

Love Is Inner Freedom

"Inner freedom" is a way of describing both a psychological dynamic within us and a spiritual value; the two are closely connected. Thérèse understood that strong feelings can hijack our goodwill and our intentions to be kind, enslaving us to our unfiltered, reactive self. Without denying the truth of our feelings, Thérèse teaches us how to act from our mature best self, our inner freedom.

The idea that managing and befriending our feelings could be part of our spiritual practice is new territory for many of us. Yet Thérèse's powerful teaching about nonviolent love makes intuitive sense: if our hearts are bitter or angry, we will find ourselves captive to feelings and powerless to make free, loving choices. The good face we try to put on it will be all on the outside.

Thérèse learned three things in particular about managing her feelings and thus maintaining inner freedom: first, her feelings could push her around and even overtake her; second, befriending her feelings could bring her back to herself; and third, managing her feelings, especially not taking things too personally, could move her into a deeper self-understanding and permit her to choose a more loving way.

Our Feelings Can Push Us Around

As she pondered the meaning of her conversion over the years, Thérèse came to a crucial insight. She noticed that her experience of her *outside* life—things that happened to her in her family or the convent—was shaped by how she was coping on the *inside*, that is, her feelings and how she interpreted them. She realized that being a loving person was connected to how she managed her feelings throughout the day: was she sad, angry, anxious, excited, or calm?

We might have heard that feelings are neither good nor bad but just are. Thérèse understood that there is a risk in that view. If she assumed that feelings just "are," without any concern for managing them, she could indulge the feelings and unintentionally hurt others. She realized that when her feelings were not excessive and when she could deal with them calmly, they were her allies and not her oppressors.

Thérèse observed, however, that sometimes *she* didn't have her feelings; the feelings had *her*. Her feelings could be problematic when someone pushed her buttons. She recalled a time from her childhood when Victoire, the household caregiver, teased her beyond her endurance. "I shouted at her and told her she was very wicked. Laying aside my customary gentleness, I stamped my foot with all my might. Poor Victoire stopped laughing."

But Thérèse's tantrum didn't last long. "After shedding tears of anger, I poured out tears of repentance, having a firm purpose of not doing it again!"[54]

Years later Thérèse encountered a situation in the convent that triggered feelings of irritation. This time she found a way to avoid acting in anger.

> I was in the laundry doing the washing in front of a Sister who was throwing dirty water into my face every time she lifted the handkerchiefs to her bench; my first reaction was to draw back and wipe my face to show the Sister who was sprinkling me that she would do me a favor to be more careful.[55]

Thérèse reflected on her anger and then made a choice: she would not make a big deal of it.

Thérèse eventually learned that an angry reaction by itself provides information. Feeling angry was an alert to her that something felt wrong or unfair. In the case of the laundry splasher, Thérèse knew that the other sister was unaware of what she was doing. If Thérèse had had a different temperament or if this particular sister were open to feedback, perhaps Thérèse could have said something. But given the realities of the moment, she made the choice to bear the annoyance.

Furthermore, Thérèse resolved not to carry a silent grudge against the clueless sister. In the peace of having let go of her angry reaction, she concludes the story by noting with gentle humor that, in the end, she was so successful that she really took a liking to the sprinkling. This episode shows that if

Thérèse recognized her anger and understood what triggered it, she could decide what to do about it.

As a child, Thérèse had learned that excessive anger could consume her, getting out of control and becoming violent. Such self-awareness comes to most children; they need not be especially brilliant or gifted. The story of Eric shows us how this can play out.

Eric's Story

A teacher with forty years of experience tells of the time she worked with a preschool group of four-year-olds. At first, the teacher said, the scene was rather chaotic; it took her several months to bring calm and order to the group. Finally the children settled down and began to really enjoy learning. The teacher could see that they took delight in the cooperative class spirit and in selecting projects from the daily curriculum.

Then one day Eric, a challenging child but one who had begun to blossom in the classroom routine, came late to class. He was in a rowdy and mean mood, purposely bumping into one of the boys and knocking over another child's work. Eric was asking for a fight, and the teacher knew she had a problem on her hands. She quickly raised her voice in a loud, forceful way, something she hadn't done in weeks.

"Stop!" she called out. "Everyone, stop! Come over here. We have a problem. Sit down for a class meeting."

The children were surprised, but they quickly moved to their usual places in the group circle. The teacher sat with them on the floor, trying to figure out what to do next.

"We have a problem, and we need to work this out," she said. "We need to do something, right now."

Then, as if confused, the teacher looked around at the seated children and said with a bit of concern in her voice, "Now, we usually have a group of nice little children in here, but a little boy just came in whom I don't recognize. Would you," and she gestured nonchalantly to Eric, "would you go outside and see if you can find Eric because I don't see him here this morning?"

Eric's eyes brightened. He scrambled up and went out of the room. The teacher had the other children return to their work, and in less than a minute, Eric was back. He closed the door carefully, and as he moved to select his project, he looked up at the teacher and said quietly to her, "I found Eric."

All was well, the teacher recounted, and the class continued without incident. At the end of the class, as Eric was leaving, he whispered to her, "I'm sorry I lost it." The teacher stooped down and hugged the little boy as he left. All really was well.

Losing and Finding Ourselves

"Losing it" refers to letting the reactive self, our natural and unfiltered feelings, take over. Like the little Thérèse who got so angry at Victoire, little Eric lost it too. The time and conditions to notice what was happening inside them gave both Thérèse and Eric the opportunity to make the choice to return to themselves.

Taking a time-out from the grip of emotions is not an academic exercise that requires advanced degrees. Even a four-year-old like Eric or the young Thérèse can do this. Coming to our best self is an intuitive, human-spiritual movement toward being genuine, being honest. Thérèse's insight confirms what psychologists today say about emotional intelligence: namely, that it is anchored in self-awareness.

As an adult, when Thérèse felt herself becoming over-whelmed, she did her best to stand her emotional ground, to hold to her inner freedom. But there were times when she was not so quick to recognize her feelings. In one instance, during Thérèse's first months in the convent, she was sorely tempted to indulge her lonely feelings by turning to the mother superior. When she had occasion to walk past the superior's door, Thérèse remarked, "I had such violent temptations to satisfy myself" that she held tight to the stairway banister in order not to turn back.[56] Thérèse knew that she was on the verge of losing emotional ground, and she made the choice to distance herself from the temptation.

Thérèse recounts a similar incident, when she was assigned to return a set of keys to the mother superior. She was glad to have this duty because she wanted a genuine excuse to see her. Another sister, knowing that the mother superior wasn't feeling well and was resting, wanted to take the keys and prevent Thérèse from entering the superior's room. But Thérèse wasn't in the mood to agree; as politely as she could, she stubbornly insisted on her duty to return the keys.

As Thérèse and the other sister went back and forth, what both of them feared came to pass: the racket they created disturbed the dozing mother superior. The other sister loudly complained that it was all Thérèse's fault. Thérèse felt herself on the verge of losing it.

> I . . . had a great desire to defend myself. Happily, there came a bright idea into my mind, and I told myself that if I began to justify myself I would not be able to retain my peace of soul.
>
> I felt, too, that I did not have enough virtue to permit myself to be accused without saying a word. My last plank of salvation was in flight. No sooner thought than done. I left without fuss, allowing the Sister to continue her discourse. . . . My heart was beating so rapidly that it was impossible for me to go far, and I sat down on the stairs in order to savor the fruits of my victory. There was no bravery there . . . ; however, I believe it was much better for me not to expose myself to combat when there was certain defeat facing me.[57]

Thérèse learned from experiences like this one that, when she felt defensiveness rising within her, she could choose to withdraw and let that particular battle pass. Leaving the situation that was causing her to lose her peace was her way of securing space in which to gain a sense of what to do. She could then return to the person or the situation calmly.

Thérèse was learning the self-management dimension of emotional intelligence.

Befriending Our Feelings

Once her feelings no longer intimidated her, Thérèse did not fight them or flee, even when she chose to step away from a conflict. Her de-escalatory approach enabled her to bear her feelings, manage her reactions, and stand her emotional ground. Instead of making her feelings into adversaries, she made friends with them, letting them help her interpret the deeper meaning of her experiences. She would extend a momentary time-out into a longer prayerful period of reflection, listening to what her feelings were telling her.

As Thérèse was preparing for her final profession as a Carmelite nun, for example, she found out that she would have to wait a bit longer for that special day. She was upset, sad, and frustrated. She did her best to listen with respect to what her feelings might be telling her, reflecting prayerfully on the commotion within.

> I found it difficult, at first, to accept this great sacrifice, but soon light shone in my soul. . . . One day, during my prayer, I understood that my intense desire to make Profession was mixed with a great self-love. Since I had *given* myself to Jesus to please and console Him, I had no right to oblige Him to do *my will* instead of His own.[58]

Accepting and even befriending her distress over the delayed date for her profession, Thérèse gained insight into the meaning of her feelings. She came to recognize two truths: one about the present and one about the past. In the present, she saw her self-love in wanting her agenda rather than God's. Reflecting more deeply, she saw as well the truth of her childhood—her need to be bonded and appreciated—still lingering. Thus Thérèse gained insight from befriending her feelings and allowing them to show her the truth of her experiences. One important lesson for Therese was her realization that she had a tendency to take everything personally.

Writing about her childhood, Thérèse remembered, "I really made a big fuss over *everything*!"[59] For Thérèse, the fuss was the indicator that her childhood vanity tended to make her focus everything on herself. In later life, she came to realize that other people often spoke from within their own dramas, their own self-concern. Noticing this, she would do her best to maintain a slight interior distance.

Thérèse adopted the discipline of not taking things personally. She was not indispensable in every situation. Others had their private stories, which were not centered on her. Patiently keeping this perspective in mind, Thérèse gently set aside her self-centeredness and allowed her best self to emerge more fully.

The more Thérèse pondered her experiences, the more she saw that she really did not need to be at war with her feelings or intimidated by them. She could confidently stand her ground emotionally or withdraw from a struggle. She could befriend her feelings, listen to what they had to tell her, and avoid taking life's ups and downs personally.

In the doorway of the superior's room, Thérèse gained insight into her control issues and her ego's needs as she encountered the sister who refused to let her have her way. She grew in the self-discipline of keeping a perspective on the larger, whole truth of her life. Over time Thérèse's attentive self-awareness made her more capable of holding on to inner freedom and making loving choices, without violence to herself or others.

This was the inner work that Thérèse did every day as she reflected on her feelings, neither ignoring nor suppressing them. The fruit of this practice showed up for other people in Thérèse's serenity and good nature. "Doing little things with great love," a phrase by which many have characterized Thérèse's spirituality, may sound unheroic and effortless, but it required Thérèse's constant willingness to be aware of her feelings, to befriend them, and to be open to what they revealed. Over the years, Thérèse emerged from the tangle of feelings, and her discovery of the role of inner freedom became an important marker of the Little Way.

Mentoring Messages for Reflection

Thérèse learned that inner freedom led her to greater self-awareness. She was better able to regulate her emotional responses and less likely to be reactive and impulsive. The emotional maturity she demonstrated gives us an example of how we too might learn to manage our feelings and make thoughtful choices about when and how to respond to others with empathy. Inner freedom is the grounding for our emotional intelligence.

✧ Recognizing what causes us to "lose it" can help us retain a free inner spirit.

Some days can get intense, and we feel overwhelmed. It's easy to imagine how that plays out. For example, if a busy mom with a demanding job finds herself stretched thin— resolving complaints from clients, working with annoying colleagues, and trying to figure out how to correct the latest program mix-up—she is primed to lose it. If on top of all that, her youngest is unruly that evening, the child stands a good chance of catching a scolding that stings with the bottled-up anger of the mother's rough day at work.

In our own ways, we have been there. We too may regret what we say or do when we are carried away by overwhelming feelings. But the road to a loving life starts with a patient and attentive respect for our feelings. It might take us a while to put our finger on just what those feelings are. Learning to pause and notice our feelings is not a onetime accomplishment; it can be a gradual stumble along the right path.

Over time we recognize the situations that push our buttons. Maybe we don't like being told what to do or what not to do. Perhaps we are impatient with the arrogant or patronizing. If we pay attention to whatever trips the switch inside us, we can learn what it feels like when we are beginning to give in to our feelings. This is the moment to take a step away from the brewing conflict.

The step might be deliberately holding our tongue, taking a breath, and letting the moment pass without lashing out. The step might be literally walking away or saying something neutral that neither aggravates the situation nor lessens it.

Managing our feelings in a spiritually and psychologically mature way asks more of us than making a mental note in passing. Self-management requires patient commitment, a reflective spirit, and regular practice. The self-discipline involved is much like the focus of a dedicated athlete, dancer, or musician.

✧ We may gain powerful perspective on our personal truth through journaling.

For many of us, the practice of journaling is an especially effective way to get in touch with our feelings and what those feelings say about us. Writing in a personal journal is not the same as recording daily activities or keeping a health log. Journaling is strictly private, so there is no need for lengthy details or self-conscious phrasing. In a journal entry, we write candidly about how we feel and what we're thinking—not every day but when the Spirit moves us, perhaps especially when we know we're dealing with turbulent emotions.

The act of writing coaxes us into naming our inner experience, sometimes in ways we hadn't registered before. As Thérèse described her autobiographical writing, "*It is like fishing with a line; I write whatever comes to the end of my pen.*"[60]

The process of writing offers discoveries and awareness. In the privacy of our journal, we can be unsparingly honest with ourselves and with God. We may find tears welling up when we name a painful loss or betrayal. The urge to write something down comes when things aren't sorted out inside. Something may bother us, something not right. At other times, the overwhelming experience of joy or gratitude may prompt us to write, or an approaching event or life transition might demand our attention.

Whatever moves us, we begin by noticing what is stirring within, responding to whatever question starts us writing, such as: Which feelings have me in their grip, pushing me around? What is that about? What is my heart's yearning?

The process of journaling for a few minutes or half an hour is a focused way to engage in the reflection that makes inner freedom possible. We come to know our personal vulnerabilities, the pain in our hearts, and the desires that fill us. We may gain honest insight into how we can do our best to love others without doing violence to our limited selves. We grow into the spacious joy of our truth in God.

Journal writing isn't for everyone. Whatever form of reflection we choose, regular practice opens our hearts to the slow work of healing on our journey to emotional and spiritual maturity.

✧ Not taking things personally is a form of emotional self-discipline that makes space for our inner freedom.

When we take things personally, we act as if whatever is going on is essentially about *us*. We put ourselves at the center of a drama someone else is creating and allow ourselves to be invaded by the feelings that have been stimulated. Perhaps we jump in and take a side in a debate that other people are having. Or we may feel flooded with excessive distress or guilt over a national or international crisis. Perhaps we get tangled up in the angry or anxious feelings of a friend or relative, forgetting that the situation they are facing is theirs, not ours.

Not taking these things personally means not letting the emotional energy of the other individual or the situation take over our inner experience. Not taking things personally means keeping an inner distance, a capacity to observe what we're feeling and to make a decision about how or whether to act.

Sometimes it's best to let go of a desire to make a big deal of something, such as the aggressive driver cutting us off on the highway or the clerk locking the store in our face, two minutes before closing time. On the other hand, if we determine that we have at least a small role to play in a situation—for example, a political issue—then we can do something that represents our values and trust others to do the same. If we find ourselves listening to another person who is dealing with many challenges, we can offer empathy and support while doing our best to keep our emotional balance.

Noticing our feelings and, when we can, taking ourselves out of the center of a drama requires patience, practice, and a willingness to not give up on ourselves. What we know from her writings is that Thérèse learned to move from being at war with her feelings, to being curious about them, to reflecting on the truths they might be telling her, and finally to creatively responding to a situation with as much self-possession as she could manage. Inner freedom is the heart quality that invites our best self to take the lead, released from the grip of any initial feelings that might arise when we are provoked or upset.

Chapter 8

Love Is Compassion

For most of us, living a loving, compassionate life is a beautiful aspiration but something that we don't think is possible in a world that includes untrustworthy people. This is a let's-be-real issue, where lovely words come up against daily friction. After all, there's not much challenge in loving those who are easy to love; it's much harder to be patient and kind, let alone compassionate, to disagreeable people. Is it even possible to stay peaceful in our hearts, respectful in our demeanor, and reasonably safe at the same time?

Thérèse took on this question, and her discoveries give us some answers. She came to understand compassion as an active, loving response to the needs and woundedness of others. For Thérèse, compassion was much more than a sympathetic gaze. Compassion was a robust and dynamic attitude of her heart, extended willingly to those she loved very much and also to those she didn't like at all.

Three aspects of Thérèse's understanding translate into life lessons for us: first, her realization that she could "invent" enemies when self-awareness was lacking; second, her awareness that she could set free her enemies—or not take enemies in the first place—by performing inconspicuous acts of compassion and empathy; third, her recognition that compassion involved setting and holding boundaries, to protect herself from those who really intended harm without succumbing to feelings of animosity.

A Discovery: We Invent Our "Enemies"

From a very young age, Thérèse felt that her vocation was to enter the convent and devote her life to God. When she entered the cloister at the age of fifteen, she embarked on a new phase of her life, outside the shelter of her home. She was full of joy about living the vocation that she had dreamed about for so long, but she wasn't spared the trials of life in a religious community.

Reality brought Thérèse up short as she experienced the challenges of community life with twenty-four older women. Her family had been a quiet nest of safe and nurturing relationships, but in the convent, Thérèse faced tension and conflict. The chores and housekeeping assignments were beyond her pampered self, and she was unprepared for the criticism she received. She had assumed that the sisters would appreciate and affirm her, encourage and help her.

In her great sensitivity, Thérèse suffered feelings of inadequacy, rejection, and hurt. She tried to be patient and kind, leaning on St. Paul's description of love in his First Letter to the Corinthians, chapter 13. But she wasn't always successful. She sometimes berated herself over her failures.

Thérèse's heart told her that the feelings of animosity that arose within her in some situations could be blocking her from the fullness of loving as Jesus calls us to love. She gained a crucial insight into compassion by mulling over one of the most challenging phrases that Jesus speaks in the Gospels: "I say to you, love your enemies" (Matthew 5:44; see Luke 6:27). Thérèse wondered how these words might apply to her, living as she did with pious women seeking holiness. With her characteristic self-awareness, she wrote, "No doubt, we don't have any enemies in Carmel, but there are feelings."[61]

Her words acknowledge the emotional reality that she experienced firsthand: even among women genuinely trying to be holy, there could be competitiveness, jealousy, hurt, distaste, and even disturbed and antagonistic behavior. Thérèse recognized that she attached the label "enemy" to those who pushed her buttons and aroused feelings of threat, revulsion, fear, or distress. She saw that, in a certain way, it was her emotional reaction that "invented" her enemy.

This was a significant realization for Thérèse. She recognized it clearly during an especially sensitive time, when her blood sister, Pauline, lost the vote for reelection as prioress of the convent. This result astonished Thérèse, who loved Pauline as deeply as her own mother. She was shocked to realize that some sisters had severely criticized her wonderful, loving Pauline! Dumbfounded at Pauline's rejection, Thérèse cried for days.

Thérèse realized that Pauline had her weaknesses as a leader; for example, she was sometimes unnecessarily strict. But in her loving heart, Thérèse registered that through their harsh criticism and gossip, the sisters had made Pauline an enemy. Their unkind words contaminated their sense of charity, violating their own values.

Thérèse had walked innocently into the important fact that personal feelings create friends as well as enemies. The favorites of some were the enemies of others. Thérèse understood more deeply how she unthinkingly created labels to sort the world into friends and foes. When she reacted with excessive feelings to the imperfections of others, she twisted them into enemies, without recognizing the defects she might have in common with them.

This, Thérèse realized, was a blind spot for her. It was the sort of thing Jesus referred to when he asked, "Why do you notice the splinter in your brother's eye, but do not perceive the wooden beam in your own?" (Luke 6:41). Thérèse saw that yes, she could and did invent enemies. It was yet another reminder that indeed, she was not perfect.

"De-Inventing" the Enemy

Gradually, Thérèse came to a second understanding: that she could free her enemies or not take them in the first place. If she could be aware of her feelings and let go of her adversarial reactions, she could retain her inner freedom. She could then act with love, even if she didn't feel love.

Having learned that her feelings invented enemies, Thérèse also learned how to "de-invent" the enemy by performing inconspicuous acts of compassion. She could take the initiative, act kindly, and let her actions help change her feelings. This was true even if she needed to set boundaries or get away for a bit in order to cope with a difficult situation.

Thérèse recognized, "Ah! what peace floods the soul when she rises above natural feelings."[62] Bringing her personal preferences and feelings of animosity to reflective prayer, Thérèse managed to see things from a different perspective. She was able to act with compassion for others instead of being a victim of her feelings of animosity.

As Thérèse practiced compassion, she came to understand its depth. She wrote, "A soul that is burning with love cannot remain inactive."[63] Compassion is neither patronizing nor manipulative. Thérèse understood compassion to be empathy combined with kindness, patience, and generosity.

In one plainspoken passage, Thérèse wrote of a sister who had "the faculty of displeasing me in everything, in her ways, her words, her character, everything seems *very disagreeable* to me."[64] So Thérèse set to work, being as kind to this sister as she could. "And when I was tempted to answer her back in a disagreeable manner, I was content with giving her my most friendly smile, and with changing the subject of the conversation."[65] The sister never gave any indication that she knew how much of a bother she was to Thérèse. Behind this simple display of kindness was Thérèse's refusal to indulge her natural feeling of repugnance.

Thérèse tried to meet people on their terms, with the relational sensitivity to notice what they needed, perhaps even before they knew it themselves. Sr. St. Pierre was a frail, cantankerous, elderly nun whom Thérèse helped each evening as they walked from prayer in the chapel to the dining room. The transit was delicate: if Thérèse moved too fast or too slowly, mishaps could occur, and Sr. St. Pierre would sharply scold her. And when they arrived at the dining room, the elder sister wanted everything arranged just so.

Thérèse noticed that Sr. St. Pierre had difficulty cutting her bread.

> With her poor crippled hands she was trying to manage with her bread as well as she could. I soon noticed this, and, each evening, I did not leave her until after I had rendered her this little service. As she had not asked for this, she was very much touched by my attention, and it was by this means that I gained her entire good graces.[66]

In this case and many others, Thérèse kept her acts of charity inconspicuous. She knew that if others notice and praise you for your charity, it's easy to become pompous about it.

Thérèse noted how natural it is to make allowances for a person with an evident physical illness but much harder to make similar allowances for the aggravating behaviors of the emotionally or mentally unwell. She grew in compassion for the more difficult personalities among the sisters. In fact, she empathized with them, for her own experience revealed how upsetting inner turmoil could be. She recognized that some of the sisters were difficult, even significantly disturbed, because they were in emotional pain. "A word, an amiable smile, often suffice to make a sad soul bloom," she noted.[67]

In response to a complaint about a troublesome sister, an enemy to some in the community, Thérèse said:

I assure you that I have the greatest compassion for Sister. If you knew her as well as I do, you would see that she is not responsible for all of the things that seem so awful to us. I remind myself that if I had an infirmity such as hers, and so defective a spirit, I would not do any better than she does, and then I would despair; she suffers terribly from her own shortcomings.[68]

Thérèse makes no effort to justify the sister's behavior. Rather, acknowledging her own vulnerability, Thérèse empathizes with the unfortunate sister, aware that if she had the same difficulties, she would do no better.

The Problem of Those Who Wish Us Harm

Although Thérèse had discovered the powerful inner dynamic with which we create enemies based on our feelings, she didn't lose touch with reality. She was well aware that on occasion, some sisters really intended to attack her and inflict pain, even if only with words and even if they thought it would be for her own good. Thérèse took action in such situations; she held her ground emotionally or set a protective boundary.

Although Thérèse never used the words "holding her ground emotionally" or "setting a boundary," her actions demonstrate these behaviors, and her reflections tell us why she used them. For example, when Thérèse wanted to return the keys but ended up creating a disturbance with the other sister, she realized that "if I began to justify myself I would not be able to retain my peace of soul."[69] So she fled, sat on the staircase, and savored her small victory, noting that it involved no bravery, just the escape from certain defeat in her desire to avoid an acrimonious exchange.

Thérèse's withdrawal certainly wasn't fight, but it also wasn't flight. The external choice to step away from a conflict was a way of remaining faithful to her commitment to love. Thérèse recognized her weaknesses and managed them as well as she could by observing boundaries.

Thérèse sensibly advises that we don't have to like our enemies in order to love them. Rather, we seek to consider them with respect and compassion. Thérèse was not wimpy in living a loving life. Her devotion was based on a deep understanding of the passion and death of Jesus.

Jesus didn't make others into enemies in his heart, but he certainly recognized that there were people who opposed him and who intended to neutralize the threat he posed to their interests. He acted in response to these threats, parrying them with creativity and compassion. When Jesus was unable to prevent violence directed toward him, he suffered the consequences with patience and love. His passion and crucifixion proved this to Thérèse.

Like Jesus, Thérèse didn't accept a threatening situation without some reflection on what her options might be. She advised others, "We should never allow kindness to degenerate into weakness."[70] She did her best to change the things she could change; when that wasn't possible, she related as she believed God would want, with patience and kindness.

Thérèse grasped the fact that a bitter or violent reaction only made a threatening situation worse. In imitation of Jesus, who showed love to his enemies, Thérèse did her best to love the good and the bad. Of course, despite her efforts, sometimes Thérèse was unsuccessful in setting or holding a protective boundary; on those occasions, she suffered from the malicious intent of others. This she accepted as the dimension of pain that attends every life that is focused on loving.

It is possible that the single greatest misconception about the spirituality of Thérèse of Lisieux, especially among women, is that she was docile and submissive, an unfortunate model of how *not* to assert oneself. That was far from the truth. What we see from her story is the strength that came from her honest self-awareness and her courage in holding her ground emotionally. In dealing with damaged and threatening people, her charity and kindness never degenerated into weakness.

Mentoring Messages for Reflection

But what about daily life in our messy, troubled world today? It would be natural for us to feel some skepticism about the idea of loving enemies and counting on boundaries to keep us safe. To unpack Thérèse's mentoring on the heart quality of compassion, we can look into what she meant by loving an enemy, setting boundaries without feelings of animosity, and loving others on their terms, not ours.

✧ Loving and "de-inventing" our enemies is inner work, starting with the intention to be respectful and kind.

Although we are wise and right to set protective boundaries for those who threaten our safety, the emotional work of "de-inventing" our enemies is very much internal. It's a result of noticing and reflecting on the feelings that arise in us.

For example, we love those who oppose us when we refuse to mock them, to express contempt, to use words that cut and belittle them. This is especially challenging in socially and politically polarized times, when we make snap judgments about whether someone is good or bad, right or wrong. Practicing restraint can be extremely challenging, and we do well to be patient with ourselves in the process, forgiving our failures and picking ourselves up to try again.

Sometimes we feel as if we face an enemy in our home, when someone we love angers us. Giving them the silent treatment or relating in an icy manner expresses hostility, not kindness. A more loving response would be to find a time when we can address the issue that has arisen with some degree of patience. It's no surprise, of course, that this kind of respect often escapes our attention, especially when we're under pressure.

The patient cultivation of an attitude of respect and compassion is a daily practice, both inside and outside the home. It is one of the small but powerful ways to guide our feet on the path of love.

✧ Compassion means setting protective boundaries without feelings of animosity.

Sometimes we encounter situations that threaten us. From Thérèse we learn that we can maintain our internal emotional integrity and avoid feelings of animosity by setting a boundary. Perhaps this means walking away from the situation. In such cases, our compassion for the other person and for ourselves is our noninvolvement, as in the example Thérèse gave of fleeing a brewing tempest.

Nonviolence is not the same as nonaction, and it certainly is not a recommendation for accepting or permitting abuse. Even when we must set a protective boundary, we don't need to hate the other, focus our contempt on them, hold violence toward them in our hearts, or intentionally hurt them. This is the essence of the insight that grew in Thérèse: she could drop the inner stance of combat and instead cultivate compassion for the other while prudently managing a boundary.

We learn a powerful lesson by observing the ways that Thérèse honored both external and internal boundaries. Externally, she practiced defusing or disengaging from conflict; internally, she registered and honored her emotional limits in order to maintain a compassionate stance.

✧ Compassion means learning to love others on their terms, not ours.

Loving others on their own terms requires emotional maturity. Small children can't do it. Even we grown-ups can't do it easily. Loving another person on their terms means choosing to pay attention to what *they* want, what *they* need, what *they* prefer. We have to understand their point of view, their context. We have to love them enough to meet them there, rather than in our own context, with our wants and preferences.

The discipline of compassion and love for the other on their terms can find its way into big and little gestures in our personal relationships. What conversation topics do we bring up when talking with a family member or a friend? As we connect, are we tuned in to their mood, their energy? How much do we assert our own needs or wants if we are dealing with a relative who is physically or mentally ill, upset, or for whatever reason just not able to respond as we might hope?

What if a friend or spouse cannot be there for us as we wish they would be? Can we recognize and make the loving choice to accept this reality, without being disappointed or holding a grudge? Can we be present in a way that respects their needs and their boundaries and brings them good?

To love others as they are, at least in this moment, may mean setting aside our own needs and preferences. Sometimes we may feel hurt, but this isn't the whole story of our love for another.

And here comes the balancing point: When is accommodating the other *not* the right thing? What boundaries should we set to honor our own reality and to love ourselves on *our* terms?

Thérèse demonstrated this idea in her efforts to be loving toward *herself*, respecting her own boundaries and needs. Despite her best intentions to act lovingly towards a particular sister she found very difficult, Therese wrote that "I used to run away like a deserter whenever my struggles became too violent."[71] She knew she had to figure out ways to respond lovingly to others that respected her own truth as well.

The stance of active compassion reveals the energy of love at the heart of the Little Way. Thérèse did little things with great love, with strong love but not harsh love. Her example mentors us wisely in the ways of the heart quality of compassion.

Chapter 9

Love Is Creativity

When we feel especially stressed by life's challenges, it's natural to yearn for escape. We plod along, doing what we must do, but we wish that the world around us were different. When it isn't, we can become frustrated.

When the "outside" route to relief appears blocked, what about the "inside" route? How can we better cope with, and sometimes even transform, our experiences, instead of assuming that we have no options? Creativity, the wellspring of inspiration, makes possible a degree of freedom, agency, and purpose in our lives, even when outside realities are daunting.

Certainly Thérèse's personal creativity showed forth in the more traditional sense, in her gifts as a painter and a writer of poems and plays. But her creativity was especially noticeable in the ways she dealt with people and circumstances. Over the years, she learned to be loving in new and unexpected ways—ways that emerged intuitively from her spirit in specific situations. The peace and joy that arose within her as she acted charitably confirmed the fact that love is inherently creative.

The Originality of Jesus

Thérèse's experience of complete conversion when she was fourteen helped her realize that she didn't have to be trapped in patterns of the past, such as rigid personal habits, cultural rules, and excessively strict religious norms. Even a subtle form of bondage was a form of violence. Jesus' path of love invited Thérèse to be flexible and innovative in meeting her own needs and those of others.

Thérèse noticed from the Gospels that legal regulations and religious habits didn't limit Jesus. He broke through conventions, offering friendship and a helping hand to people who were considered outcasts, undeserving, or of no importance. Jesus proclaimed the unique, surprising message that love of God and love of neighbor are enough. He didn't propose new laws but advocated a new attitude of love. He spoke of new life in the Holy Spirit, the endlessly creative, nurturing Spirit of love who is present in each of our hearts, the Spirit who animates all human life.

Thérèse observed how original Jesus was in his use of parables, in his ways of healing, and in his responses to difficult situations. His spontaneous replies often flustered his questioners, disarmed his adversaries, and simply amazed the crowd. His priorities even surprised his family and disciples. Thérèse noticed the fresh, loving directness with which he engaged with his world. His example, along with her awareness that God was continuously merciful and creative in her own life, encouraged her.

In her younger years, however, Thérèse wasn't always spontaneous and confident in making creative choices. Beginning when she was twelve years old, she suffered for a year and a half from what religious teachers call scrupulosity: an obsessive, unwarranted concern that her thoughts and tendencies were imperfect and sinful and that she didn't always act according to the rules. She was especially concerned about vanity, frightened, for example, by "the joy I had putting on some pretty sky-blue ribbons Aunt had given me for my hair."[72] This innocent sensual thrill so disturbed the scrupulous Thérèse that she "confessed . . . even this childish pleasure which seemed to be a sin to me."[73]

In her desire to be good and to be holy, Thérèse internalized an unreasonably strict understanding of what was sinful and what was not. She needed to grow into her creativity.

Benefiting from the guidance of her older sister Marie and her own habit of prayerful reflection, Thérèse was able to free herself from scrupulosity. In her mid-teens, she increasingly became her own person. Writing about that time in her life, Thérèse observed, "Freed from its scruples and its excessive sensitiveness, my mind developed."[74]

As Thérèse grew out of the timidity of her scrupulous phase, she found herself willing to speak and act with increasing confidence. She relied more and more on her own inner sensitivities, acting with a good deal of inner authority and creativity. Although respectful, she was less and less encumbered by the expectations of others.

Thérèse did all this with an appropriate disregard for general opinion, conventional wisdom, and authoritative directives.

Her account of a group pilgrimage to Rome at the age of fourteen brings this creativity to life.

The Trip to Rome

In Thérèse's telling, the pilgrimage to Rome involved quite a few instances of minor transgressions on her part. She wandered, enthralled by the art, into monastic cloisters that forbade the presence of women. She reached through grates to touch protected holy relics. She climbed through fences at the Colosseum so that she could kiss the earth where the martyrs died. Remembering these moments, she wrote with amusement, "I still cannot understand why women are so easily excommunicated in Italy, for every minute someone was saying: 'Don't enter here! Don't enter there, you will be excommunicated!'"[75]

To be excommunicated is to be ousted from the Church community. Thérèse clearly saw the absurdity of that threat for such insignificant infractions.

The young pilgrim demonstrated her sense of inner authority and creative personal initiative when she held her own in an audience with the pope. On that special day, the pilgrimage group walked solemnly through the awe-inspiring majesty of the Vatican to the hall where they were to personally greet Pope Leo XIII. Each pilgrim was to kneel before the pope, kiss his ring, and receive his blessing in reverent silence.

When it came her turn to pay her respects, Thérèse, unexpectedly and against the rules, spoke up confidently in the hushed room. To shocked, stifled gasps from the pilgrims around her, she earnestly asked the pope for permission to enter the Carmel as a religious sister, even though the clerical superior of the Lisieux convent had said she was too young.

Caught off guard, the pope responded noncommittally, "Do what the superiors tell you." The pope spoke a theological truth, of course, but Thérèse, undeterred, spoke a very practical truth: resting her hands on his knees, she said, "Oh! Holy Father, if you say yes, everybody will agree!"

Now taking notice, the pope gazed steadily at this audacious young woman. He said, this time with deliberate emphasis, "Go. . . . *You will enter if God wills it.*"[76]

Thérèse felt encouraged that the Holy Father had spoken to her, but she also felt terribly let down by his cautious words. She made ready to speak to him again, but two guards tapped her politely, signaling her to rise. When she didn't get up, they lifted her up by her arms as the pope raised his hand to bless her. The guards literally carried her to the door, where they gave her a souvenir medal of the pope and then ushered her unceremoniously on her way.

Thérèse's breach of protocol was so extraordinary that it made the local papers. But despite this and her great disappointment, Thérèse was at peace with what she had done. She was confident that she had acted on what she believed to be God's will.

Her creative initiative turned out well in the end. Even though Thérèse didn't succeed in getting a direct endorsement from Pope Leo XIII, the ecclesial superiors who were present at the audience were impressed by this evidence of her sincere desire to become a Carmelite sister. In a few weeks, she received the permission she needed. Thérèse entered Carmel within the next six months.

Creativity in Convent Life

Entering the Carmelite community fulfilled a dream for Thérèse, but it came with the aforementioned frictions of daily life in the community. Doing her best to cope with her new situation, the young Thérèse displayed a proper spirit of obedience and mature judgment as she sought creative, loving solutions to difficult moments. She had a good sense for when a typical, usually helpful norm could be disregarded in favor of a more responsive, creative action.

On one occasion, she was with the sisters during a time of quiet prayer. One sister inadvertently kept up an annoying clicking noise, destroying Thérèse's quiet prayer despite her efforts to ignore it. "I had a great desire to turn my head and stare at the culprit who was very certainly unaware of her 'click.'"[77]

In fact, casting a dirty look may have been the conventional thing to do, even in that pious situation, but Thérèse decided such a response would not be loving. It wouldn't help the prayer that Thérèse had planned for herself, since she would have to bear feelings of regret and guilt. And a dirty look would certainly not help the prayer of the clicking sister either.

Searching for a way to manage her annoyance, Thérèse relaxed her boundaries and let go of her personal expectations. In a stroke of mini-genius that may have surprised even herself, she flipped the annoyance over: the noise that had been destroying her prayer of quiet became the focus of her prayer.

God's grace surged in her spirit, and she created a "concert" out of the aggravating sound.

Some years later, with ironic humor, she described the situation: "[M]y prayer (which was not the *Prayer of Quiet*) was spent in offering this concert to Jesus."[78]

Additional challenges confronted Thérèse when she became responsible for mentoring new members of the community. She responded with great creativity to the unique temperament and specific needs of each sister, adapting her corrections and directives appropriately. "Some of them I have to catch by the scruff of the neck," Thérèse said to her sister Pauline, "others by their wingtips."[79]

With some sisters she was stern and with others empathetic, always tuned to what would most help the sister. She directed one of them who cried frequently and copiously to collect all her tears in a tiny mussel shell that Thérèse provided. The ridiculousness of this solution soon cured the sister.

Sometimes Thérèse's creativity showed up in the playful spirit with which she spoke of matters that were usually treated with unquestioning deference. For example, she often expressed a desire to be a priest, despite knowing that the Catholic Church did not ordain women. She respected the priesthood, but she wasn't intimidated by traditional strictures. In a conversation with her sister Céline after Thérèse had become ill with tuberculosis, she said, perhaps with a touch of humor,

> The good God is taking me to heaven *before* the age when ordination usually takes place; He must want to spare me the chagrin of witnessing the actual frustration of my ardent desire to be a priest.[80]

At another time, writing of all the vocations to which she had aspired—apostle, doctor, crusader, martyr, priest—Thérèse wrote, "But alas! while desiring to be a *Priest*, I admire and envy the humility of St. Francis of Assisi and I feel the *vocation* of imitating him in refusing the sublime dignity of the *Priesthood*."[81] In her free and imaginative way, Thérèse was both able to envision herself as a priest and willing to accept the reality of her calling to be a Carmelite sister.

Creative Nonviolence

Thérèse didn't develop a life of loving creativity just because it was a nice idea or personally fulfilling or because it helped her score points in the community. She actually found no other good choice. She was determined to avoid an adversarial attitude and violence toward herself and others, and she noticed that most of the commonsense ways of reacting to difficult people were also violent.

Thérèse saw sisters trying to overcome their imperfections by performing harsh personal penance; in fact, they seemed to compete with one another in penitential practices. Thérèse had tried these practices too. Eventually, she realized that she had no capacity for punitive mortifications, and she recognized the inherent violence in what were intended to be pious acts. She also observed how even good people could turn to gossip or give a sister the silent treatment if they had been offended. To remain loving, Thérèse would have to be open to new possibilities. She came to trust in the spirit of God's love in her heart.

Thérèse tried to use her creativity especially in circumstances of tension or conflict. She recognized that if she was not going to engage in a fight, she might get stepped on or mistreated. She was clearly aware of the many ways that she and others in the convent could be bullied or taken advantage of by those intent on getting their own way.

Thérèse's solutions were sometimes barely noticed. Often she was content to wait patiently as a drama played out, without being drawn into taking sides. The choice for nonengagement was itself a creative response.

Thérèse was not always successful in her attempts to offer a creative response to a tense situation. As we have seen, at some moments the only loving thing was to leave the scene entirely. She wrote of an interaction she had with a disturbed sister, the one she had earlier described as completely disagreeable to her. Subjected to sheer outrage by this sister, Thérèse could not manage her feelings; she knew she couldn't handle the situation with kindness. To avoid the sister's invectives, Thérèse simply fled.

A short time before this crisis, a calm and in-charge Thérèse had volunteered to work with this particular sister, precisely because none of the other sisters could manage being with her. Now, however, *Thérèse* could not manage either! In this moment, she was no more emotionally capable than the sister whose outrage she fled. She later wrote that she thought herself a traitor, totally inadequate to her ideal of holiness.

But Thérèse *wasn't* a traitor. She had indeed failed in her ideal of being able to interact in a kindly way. Thinking of herself as a traitor would be only a further failure, a failure to be kind and loving to herself. Thérèse was not perfect, but her inadequacies weren't irredeemable. They were opportunities for a creative response.

Thérèse's relentless willingness to be in a kind and noncombative relationship with this troublesome sister eventually had a positive effect. One day at recreation, the sister asked her, "Would you tell me, Sister Thérèse of the Child Jesus, what attracts you so much toward me; every time you look at me, I see you smile?" Thérèse responded that it was because she was happy to see her, diplomatically noting in her autobiography that "it is understood that I did not add that this was from a spiritual standpoint."[82]

When she was her own best self, Thérèse could see the best in the sister too, from God's standpoint. Then Thérèse was at peace and happy. Her smile was honest and kind, not fake.

People with different gifts from those of Thérèse will probably take their own approach to difficult interpersonal relationships. Someone might access their creativity by delivering immediate, assertive feedback that could lead the offending person to modify their behavior. Although Thérèse did speak up forcefully on occasion, this was rare. Most of her stories show us that direct confrontation was not Thérèse's gift.

Thérèse did what she could within her capacities. Her gift of creatively thinking outside the normal ways, tapping into a spirit of love, effected positive changes. She made immediate, creative choices in situations she could handle. When she felt overwhelmed, her creative, nonviolent response was to withdraw. She would return, when possible, in reconciliation.

What these examples have in common is that Thérèse felt empowered to make choices based on how God would want her to act. She didn't give undue weight to the "shoulds" and "oughts" that so often govern our responses.

Mentoring Messages for Reflection

Social expectations about proper behavior can get in our way sometimes. These norms may help us be polite and look good, but they may also trap us in our ingrained patterns. Thérèse's model is particularly freeing for those of us who tend to equate goodness with compliance to rules. She shows us how to be creative in loving.

Even as a young girl, Thérèse recognized that sometimes a norm might not need to be observed. In this respect, she may have benefited from being the youngest child; elder children seem more likely to follow the rules. Unfortunately, the unspoken rules in our families, our workplaces, and our cultures can shut down new possibilities of the moment. Our imaginations fail us.

We might unconsciously *prefer* to get trapped in our complacency if the issue before us involves injustice to others. We recognize that there may be risks to us if we step forward. No matter what problem or opportunity the outside world presents to us, the bindings that keep us stuck in unimaginative and perhaps damaging patterns are usually within.

What to do? As we look to Thérèse's example, two takeaways suggest themselves. The first has to do with how creativity grows.

⬦ Loving creativity can't be scripted, but it can be nurtured.

Creativity arises gradually, intuitively, spontaneously as we learn to trust the movement of the Spirit in our hearts. The experience of a young man named Jayson gives us a glimpse of how we can nurture the heart quality of creativity as we grow in self-awareness and confidence.

When Jayson was a middle school student in an impoverished and violence-wracked community, the rigid, unspoken rules of his tough-guy world kept him silent and afraid when the local bully teased or hit the weaker kids. He felt shame and anger, but he was locked into the rules about how guys should behave, afraid to draw attention to himself by standing up for the weaker ones. He felt guilty and stuck.

Inclined to be reflective, Jayson gained useful perspective as he grew older. As a teenager and then a young adult, he realized that a lot of things he feared didn't actually happen. Without losing the street smarts that alerted him to risky situations, he didn't let a dicey moment keep him imprisoned in silent fear.

With a greater sense of flexibility and the conviction that he had options, Jayson often managed to head off a conflict or de-escalate it. He gained confidence in his ability to distract or even engage with an aggressive person, and this confidence gave him a calming presence. This was especially true as he realized that a threat often came from someone who was troubled or perhaps mentally ill.

Along with having more compassion, Jayson grew in the heart quality of creativity. As an adult, he became a community activist and an insightful writer, helping others understand how to address injustice, racism, and sexism.

We can see in Jayson's story the importance of his habit of observation and reflection. We can also note close connections among three of the heart qualities of Thérèse's Little Way: Jayson's active *creativity* flowed from his deepening *compassion* and his growing sense of *inner freedom*.

Jayson realized too that creativity in real life can't be scripted. Loving creativity emerges spontaneously and intuitively in the present moment, if we are open to the inspirations of our hearts. We can think about the possibilities in an upcoming situation, and this might help us be more open. But creativity usually arises unprompted. It involves not an ego-driven calculation but an intuitive response in the moment.

The creativity in our responses may not be evident to us until after an event, when we reflect on what has happened. We act in the flow of a situation, often surprising ourselves and knowing in retrospect that it was the best we could have done. Self-consciousness in the moment clogs our creative juices!

Think of the skilled athlete: the baseball or tennis player, the gymnast. They surely pay close attention to proper form during practice drills. But thinking too much about what they are doing in the intensity of a match could be the path to failure.

True creativity, especially creative love, has a quality of spontaneity and genuineness that flows effortlessly to the present moment. This may be our surest sign of the sacred within our ordinary daily lives. It is what Christians call the inspiration of the Holy Spirit. In our unscripted, day-to-day attempts to be more loving, we move within the generative power of God's love and participate in his ongoing work of creation.

A willingness to try something new is a second takeaway from Thérèse's mentoring in creativity.

✧ With patience and caring, we might see an opportunity to put creativity in motion.

What we can see in Thérèse's stories is that her overriding intention to avoid violence and show kindness led her to some unconventional solutions, such as treating the clicking sound during prayer time as a little concert. Since she couldn't ignore the irritating sound, she befriended it and so restored a sense of peace in her heart.

In the language of psychology, the heart quality of creativity that Thérèse displayed in her life is closely related to the notions of agency, initiative, and authorization. Thérèse learned from personal experience that situations could be changed for the better when she took action, even if that action was as subtle as extending a gracious smile or a friendly word or as adjusting her internal expectations. Similar to the dynamic of inner freedom, the spirit of creativity flowed from Thérèse's confidence and her willingness to put herself into play in a given situation.

Thérèse didn't have the gift of verbal assertiveness, which might have enabled her to give others feedback and help them modify their behavior. She did have the gift of internal authority and a sense of personal power in her ways of engaging with others. Her actions might have been viewed from the outside as signs of simple kindness, but from the inside, they represented conscious choices to refrain from unloving responses and create new possibilities.

A contemporary example demonstrates the power of innovative creativity. In this case, the initiative of a theme park staffer made all the difference for a distressed family with an autistic child.

The family was enjoying a long-planned trip to a popular amusement park. The day was long, and by late afternoon, they were getting tired. The child had managed himself well up to that point, but then disaster struck. The special final ride, the one he had been looking forward to all day, was closed for maintenance. The frustrated child fell to the ground in an uncontrollable fit of anger and weeping.

The overwrought parents despaired of soothing the child. Then a nearby staff member gently laid down on the ground by the child, talking softly to the boy until he calmed down. No one had taught the worker how to do this, but she instinctively, intuitively, and without self-consciousness moved to connect with the boy. Her creative, spontaneous compassion calmed him, and he cheered up even more when he received a special souvenir and a return voucher.

We might find ourselves facing a situation that we don't know how to handle. If we are willing to be proactive, to take creative initiative, and to move toward the good, something may shift, and life-giving possibilities can arise. This is the creativity of nonviolent love. It is the movement of the transcendent spirit of the loving God within us.

This spirit of creativity gives us hope that the future will not just repeat the past. Creative love cultivates the growth of new possibilities, sometimes with just a word or a smile.

Chapter 10

Love Is a Willing Spirit

Most of us aren't taught much about how to use our human will. Conventional wisdom considers willpower a good thing. We admire heroes who have a can-do attitude, the folks who are able to power through. The culture fails to warn us how easily selfish willfulness can dominate these proactive attitudes.

This chapter examines Thérèse's experience of her willpower and some of her early ambivalence about this aspect of her personality. It looks at the critical distinction between *willingness* and *willfulness*. This may look like hair splitting. But a willing spirit unlocks enormous energy for good, while willfulness can lead us to bully ourselves or others.

A Strong Will

We know from Thérèse's autobiography and from her mother's writings that the child Thérèse was strong-willed and stubborn. Although she was usually sweet, she also threw tantrums and lost her temper. On another occasion when she became angry with her caregiver, Victoire, for teasing her, Thérèse loudly denounced her with the worst expletive she could summon: "Victoire, you are a brat!"[83]

Similarly, when Thérèse and her sister were invited to choose some fabric, yarn, and similar items from a basket, the little Thérèse grasped the entire basket and declared, "I choose all!"[84] Thérèse was not a weak-willed little girl by any means. And she recognized the power of her will, even as a child.

Later in her youth, Thérèse sometimes prayed that God would take away her freedom. She had heard stories of saints who asked God to take their intellect and will, and this became her prayer as well. She thought that without her freedom, the power of her will would be reduced, and she would be cured of stubbornness. But of course she was misguided in these ideas. God could not take away Thérèse's freedom; her free will was a core gift of her personhood.

Thérèse knew firsthand that her will gave her power to take action but could become an out-of-control force that got her into trouble. Over the course of her life, she gained a deeper understanding of her will and an appreciation for its positive energy. She saw that her will could be a source of strength, giving her the energy for decision-making, determination, drive, courage, and desire.

At the same time, Thérèse understood the negative potential of the will. She saw that a spirit of determination could lead to rigidity and that drive and desire could be corrupted into drivenness and self-centered, excessive passion. She recognized that using willpower selfishly could overpower others; there was a difference between being courageous and being contentious.

Reflecting on her own experience, Thérèse recognized that there are different ways to engage the power of the will, and not all of them are along the path of love. She could get her selfish way by willfulness; she also could accommodate others in charity by approaching them with a willing spirit. She understood, as she matured, that the saints didn't actually want to be rid of their will but to be healed of their willfulness.

Willing or Willful: A Distinction

Thérèse first glimpsed the spirit of willingness as she reflected on her complete conversion. She wrote that her contribution to that transformative moment was "my *good will*, which was never lacking."[85] "*Bonne volonté*" is the phrase Thérèse uses, which translates as "good will."

In English, "good will" usually means "sincerity or honesty." But in this specific instance, Thérèse clearly means that her will was focused on open receptivity, a welcoming willingness to accept God's will. She wasn't locked into a self-centered, resistant willfulness.

Reflecting on the experience of her Christmas conversion, Thérèse recognized that until then, she had been in bondage to her excessive feelings while bullying herself to be a perfect little girl. She came to see the violence of her own willfulness, her insistent drivenness to please, no matter what. In retrospect, Thérèse recognized that her liberation had been possible because of her good will—that is, her willingness to recognize and accept the sheer grace of the moment.

Thérèse's insights into the spirit of willingness deepened as she read the Gospels and noticed how Jesus was never willful, never coercive, in what he did or said. This baffled the disciples on those occasions when they expected him to use aggressive force. Think of the time they suggested calling down fire and brimstone on the Samaritans who refused to offer them hospitality. Jesus rebuked the disciples and continued on his way (see Luke 9:52-56).

Again, when soldiers came to arrest Jesus, the disciples' first instinct was to draw swords. One of them sliced off the ear of the high priest's servant. "Stop, no more of this!" Jesus said (Luke 22:51). Jesus made himself available to help others, heal, preach, and give life. Ultimately, at his crucifixion, he offered patient love in the face of lethal violence.

Pondering the way of Jesus, Thérèse changed for the better what she was able to change. And she practiced patience when she encountered obstacles she could not move.

Unveiling Mixed Motives

In her determination to gain permission to join the Carmelite community, the teenage Thérèse demonstrated great tenacity. She proactively sought the support of all the key people in the chain of authority, up to and including the pope. Perhaps because becoming a Carmelite was an object of such passion for Thérèse, she was crushed when the authorities told her that yes, she could enter, but no, not right now. Thérèse would have to wait three more months.

This decision to delay Thérèse's entrance may have been intended to protect her fragile health from the rigors of the community's Lenten ascetical practices and the winter conditions of the barely heated convent. Thérèse received the decision, however, as a personal rejection. Her initial reaction was a form of willful inner tantrum. "At first the thought came into my mind not to lead a life as well regulated as had been my custom."[86]

In other words, she was tempted to sabotage her own preparation for the convent while she waited. This petulant, self-pitying reaction would have been an echo of her childhood stubbornness, undermining what she really wanted.

Over the next days, however, Thérèse recognized her mixed motives. She saw her willfulness at work in trying to control the situation. She had lost her inner freedom; her willpower was in "willful" mode. By acting in irritation and retaliation, she would harm only herself. She regained her inner freedom and willingly accepted this disappointment. "[S]oon I understood the value of the time I was being offered," she wrote.[87] Instead of indulging in resentment, Thérèse resolved to give herself over to serious preparation.

Thérèse never fully outgrew this tendency to hold tight to her own idea of what should be happening and overreact when her plans were frustrated. She exhibited the same impatient reaction later in her religious life, when a different delay presented itself. But the better she came to know herself, the more prepared she was to drop her controlling attitude and abide a situation with a willing spirit.

Thérèse came to see in willfulness the seeds of self-violence. Willfulness breeds a sense of being unfree and driven, a compulsion to dominate and overwhelm, even coercively, any opposition. In her willfulness, Thérèse saw, she was a slave to her feelings. She knew firsthand how readily her willpower could take over and dominate her behavior. She knew how vulnerable she was to bullying herself and others.

Willingness Is Courageous

Over and over, the strong-willed Thérèse reflected on her experiences with a perceptive sensitivity as to whether she was pushing her own agenda—that is, willfully grasping tightly to her own ideas—or acting with an appropriate combination of desire and detachment, a willing spirit. When she took on the responsibility of guiding young members in the community, her new role refined this capacity. Initially seeing her mentoring task as "beyond my strength," Thérèse took courage from her realization that, with trust in God, all things are possible. She stepped fully into her duties.

> One feels it is absolutely necessary to forget one's likings, one's personal conceptions, and to guide souls along the road which Jesus has traced out for them without trying to make them walk one's own way. [88]

Thérèse confronted novices' weaknesses gently and firmly, without fostering in them a striving for perfection rooted in willfulness and violence. She accepted calmly the occasional complaints of new members that she was strict with them, not taking their criticism personally. Wisely, Thérèse refrained from consoling them if their feelings were hurt by her straight talk.

Thérèse on one occasion displayed a quiet and forceful anger in response to a situation that she saw as unjust: a delay imposed on one of the novices for the taking of her vows. The decision was a power play on the part of the mistress of novices, Thérèse's superior, and its motives were self-centered. Thérèse spoke up during a community discussion when some of the sisters noted that the superior had the right to delay vows "as a trial." Thérèse sharply retorted, "There are some trials that should not be given."[89] There was an edge in her voice that caught everyone's attention because she didn't usually express herself with such vehemence.

Thérèse's disagreement was honest, blunt, and forceful, but not divisive or adversarial. She later spoke to the superior, who agreed with Thérèse and dropped the imposed delay.

As Thérèse taught new members of the convent, she had some concern that her emphasis on the free internal act of accepting situations that could not be changed would be confused with passivity. She emphasized to the young sisters that she did her best to address difficult situations in loving, creative ways. When she could not change something, she willingly endured it and sought to remain kind. Her endurance was not passivity.

Even during the truly dreadful experiences of her final illness, as she succumbed to tuberculosis, Thérèse was willingly patient with herself and good-natured with others. That willing spirit could never be confused with giving up. A spirit of willingness was the invisible core of her emotional and spiritual courage.

Mentoring Messages for Reflection

From Thérèse we can learn how to step away from bullying ourselves and others. She helps us understand the way of courageous, willing action that is neither passive nor coercive. A willing spirit is the heart quality that provides energy for an active, loving life. There are useful life lessons here that help us grow in our personal power without the pressure of perfectionism.

✧ We don't lose our willpower when we cultivate a willing spirit; we change it.

Finding an appropriate relationship between our will and our power is a major task of adulthood, especially in the workplace. It is particularly complicated for young people who are just finding their confident voice and for those who face barriers of racism or sexism in their quest to establish their authority.

The majority of books, leadership theories, and executive coaches in the mainstream culture make the assumption that we are most effective in our professional and personal lives when we claim our power and confidently assert our agency. The distinction between *willfulness* and *willingness* never comes up. If it did, there would probably be a negative view of the notion that we can be open and willing to respond to a situation without having a predetermined position. Clearly, the heart quality of a willing spirit that Thérèse cultivated is a countercultural value.

The distinction between a *willful* spirit and a *willing* spirit is a subtle one that does not erase the value of our will but enriches it. Thérèse learned that when we cultivate an attitude of willingness, we don't lose our willpower, but we change it. Willingness is focused energy balanced with receptivity and self-surrender to God's providence regarding what we can and can't do.

For Thérèse, willingness was actively welcoming and engaging God's providence as she found it in each moment, no matter whether it was pleasant or difficult. Willingness had nothing to do with powerlessness, defeatism, or victimhood. Willingness was creatively taking charge, not at the level of self-centeredness, but at the depths of what she believed she could do, without violence, in a situation. A willing spirit allowed Thérèse to use her personal freedom to make a loving choice.

In our own lives, especially in our areas of responsibility, a willing spirit can manifest authentic passion, resolve, determination, and power. It's not ego driven. It flows from self-awareness, detachment, nonviolence, creativity, and compassion.

T. S. Eliot said, "The last temptation is the greatest treason: to do the right deed for the wrong reason."[90] Thérèse had the intuition that perhaps a greater treason is to do the right thing for the right reason but in the wrong way—a way that is willful, coercive, bullying, or overbearing. Her insights about willfulness and willingness became some of Thérèse's most important lessons in the science of love.

✧ Leadership with a willing spirit means letting go of the energy of coercion.

It's possible to square Thérèse's guidance about a willing spirit with the cultural value of getting things done, although it means letting go of coercion and domination. Myra's story offers an example of the nuances involved.

Myra, a leader in an urban farming project, is what we might call a can-do person. She has real passion for greening her community, and she's gifted with stamina, grit, and persistence. Thérèse's mentoring can warn Myra away from using coercion to get things done.

If Myra approaches her community project with a driving intensity that railroads others, her enthusiasm can turn into willfulness and coercion. An adversarial spirit can creep in, throwing a shadow over the project. Willful force can violate the potential for harmony and creativity in the neighborhood group, demeaning the opinion and pace of others. Such willfulness also can harm Myra, who might burden herself with excessive commitments and thus be violent with herself.

On the other hand, if Myra approaches her project with her usual high level of commitment and energy but with openness to the views and creativity of others and to the unexpected things that come up, then her perseverance becomes a gift of her willing spirit. If she is intentional about wanting to collaborate with others, Myra will need to anticipate and manage her personal tilt toward being pushy. When her enthusiasm comes from an inner freedom that is paired with a genuine receptivity to the realities that other people care about—that is, when she is also compassionate—she is more likely to put her creative energy toward problem-solving while keeping other people committed to the project. A willing spirit will make a successful project more likely, even if it may be a bit slower paced or different in nature from her initial vision.

Myra's project is one that will work best if she can tap collaborative energies. But perhaps in our workplace or in public service, we find ourselves responsible for implementing projects that are difficult, controversial, or divisive. Sometimes a willing spirit must be put to the task of leading others in efforts that they would rather not pursue. Mature leadership can establish requirements that must be met in the real world while avoiding the disrespect and coercion that result from succumbing to a willful spirit. We can bring to the table a willing spirit that requires accountability, as Thérèse did in mentoring the novices.

✧ Willfulness and perfectionism together are a recipe for spiritual violence. The irony is that we can't make ourselves be less willful.

For Myra and for us, there is a close relationship between perfectionism and willfulness. If we set out to be perfect high achievers, then our thoughts, words, and actions commandeer us and, through us, commandeer others. Willfully resolving to work at perfection is a disguised form of self-centered ambition. It's a recipe for spiritual and psychological violence.

We might notice subtly violent behaviors in ourselves as we power through a day's obligations. In our quiet reflection at the end of the day, we might recognize that we have operated from a will-*full* spirit. Self-awareness can help us put on the brakes, regain our inner freedom, and be our best self.

In willingness we take a deep breath and relax a bit, unclench. We examine honestly the spirit in which we work, love, and play every day. Over time this self-awareness can gentle our spirit and soften our attitudes.

There is a balancing act here: we can act with a willing spirit without relinquishing the energy of our willpower. When we do, we become less coercive and feel more alive. Even subtle violence in thoughts and feelings can fall away. When we put aside compulsion, anxiety, and striving, we can find peace, balance, and patience.

We never get perfect at this; some degree of willfulness is more often than not a subtle ingredient in our motivation and activity. The supreme irony, of course, is that we can't will-fully rid ourselves of willfulness! Cultivating a willing spirit is a lifelong process, and we must rely on the mystery of grace to pursue it. We need to be patient and kind to ourselves in our imperfections, even in our inability to be perfectly willing.

Chapter 11

Love Is Gratefulness

The heart quality of gratefulness, one of the hallmarks of Thérèse's Little Way, may sound a bit trite at first. Isn't it natural for most of us to feel thankful for the good things we are blessed to have? There are any number of self-help practices that emphasize the value of nurturing a spirit of gratefulness.

For Thérèse, however, a spirit of gratefulness was an all-encompassing appreciation for the *whole* of life. Thérèse's gratitude was for the painful moments along with the joyful. Hers was a fundamental all-encompassing stance that faced and accepted reality with a genuine trust that love would have the last word.

How did Thérèse grow into this transforming attitude of gratefulness? We find an answer by tracing her unfolding understanding of the mystery of God's love in her life. In her autobiography, Thérèse repeatedly expresses her intense desire to love God and to be loved by God. "I understand so well that it is only love that makes us acceptable to God."[91]

Thérèse knew from her youngest years that true joy and gratitude were anchored in a loving relationship with God. "I loved God very much and offered my heart to Him very often, making use of the little formula Mother had taught me."[92] She pondered the mystery of the words "to love God." It was a phrase that came to her easily as a child, but later in her life, she came to wonder what exactly it might mean.

Thérèse knew that to love God is to love all that God loves, and in the kind and patient way that God loves. She understood *"that Charity is the EXCELLENT WAY that leads most surely to God."*[93] But she wondered if there was a more focused and directly personal way to understand loving God.

Thérèse's insights into loving God deepened through three developmental phases. In emotionally tender incidents of her childhood, she focused her love of God on obedience. Then, as a teenager, she embraced the more passionate desire for intimacy with God that characterized her youthful Carmelite vocation. Finally, in the maturity of her convent life, especially in the years immediately prior to her death, her love for God flowed from and led back to a profound gratefulness.

Pleasing God through Obedience

From the age of two and a half until her complete conversion just before her fourteenth birthday, Thérèse focused on love of God primarily by pleasing God and, in particular, by being perfectly obedient and charitable. Her idea of loving God was modeled on her way of loving her parents, trying to please them by doing their bidding. She also imitated the devotional practices of her parents and sisters, trying hard to achieve goodness and be holy.

Her mother, Zélie Martin, wrote of Thérèse, "The little one is our whole happiness. She will be good; one can already see the germ of goodness in her. She speaks only about God and wouldn't miss her prayers for anything."[94]

Thérèse knew that Jesus had said that obedience was important. He told his disciples that those who love God will keep his commandments (see John 14:15). The lives of the saints, which her father read regularly to the family, emphasized the value of obedience as well.

Part of the revelation of Thérèse's complete conversion, however, was recognizing her mixed motives. She saw that she had acted charitably and been obedient not only to love God but also to look good, to be recognized as a perfect little girl. When no one noticed her virtue, she cried. Her conversion jolted her into awareness that she had been practicing virtue "in a strange way."[95] She would never love God perfectly through simple obedience.

It wasn't that Thérèse needed to give up obedience; rather, she needed to purify her motives as much as she could. By gaining more insight into the limits of obedience as a primary way of expressing love, she moved into a second phase in her desire to love God.

Seeking Intimacy with God

When she entered the convent, Thérèse looked forward to a life of prayerful intimacy with God, her Beloved. She continued to pursue proper obedience and acts of charity, but now her desire centered more on her longing to reach out and grasp God in an intimate relationship. The psalms she recited at Carmel informed her prayer. She sought God as did the deer thirsting for running streams and the parched earth seeking moisture.

> As the deer longs for streams of water,
> so my soul longs for you, O God. (Psalm 42:2)

> O God, you are my God—
>   it is you I seek!
> For you my body yearns;
>   for you my soul thirsts,
> in a land parched, lifeless,
>   and without water. (Psalm 63:2)

In Thérèse's desire to grasp God, there was a dimension of possessing God as a treasured object. Her longing held an element of controlling, and her yearning for God a quality of self-preoccupation and willfulness. She was trying to take hold of God on her terms. She wasn't considering God's terms.

Two years after she entered Carmel, during her private retreat preparing for her investiture into the community, Thérèse wrote to her sister Pauline. She began by lamenting that Jesus was not responding to her. She could bear the spiritual aridity but told her sister, "[T]here is something, I don't know what, that repels me" about some of the sisters she was living with. Jesus' silence was a problem, and the difficult sisters were a problem, but she was "VERY *happy*, happy to suffer what Jesus wants me to suffer."[96]

Thérèse said she was happy, but she didn't speak of the peace and joy of the soul that were the usual intuitive indicators of her true path. She was experiencing, rather, a driven sense of obligatory happiness. Peace and joy she received from God; happiness was an experience for which she was reaching. She reached too far. She didn't want "Jesus to have any sorrow," she wrote; she wanted to "convert *all* the sinners of this earth and to save all the souls in purgatory!"[97] Thérèse perhaps proclaimed too much, desired too much.

In later life, Thérèse would express similar sentiments in prayers and poems, and these would ring with personal truth and authenticity. But at sixteen years of age, Thérèse was in the grip of normal adolescent idealism. Her words reveal a subtle desire to be in charge and to achieve her own will, her own vision of how to love God. "I would so much like to Love Him. . . . Love Him more than He has ever been loved!"[98]

Passionate as she was, Thérèse didn't recognize the undercurrent of grandiosity in such a desire. She was still growing into the subtle awareness that loving God is not a contest. She didn't notice that her loving was aimed at possessing God. With the energy of her strong will, Thérèse aspired to do whatever was necessary to acquire a sense of union with her Beloved.

God transformed Thérèse's idealism through the crucible of suffering that was about to begin. She grew frustrated in her efforts to grasp the God for whom she longed. Instead of blissful intimacy with God, she more often experienced aridity and boredom as she prayed. She felt the silence of God. As Thérèse imagined it, "Jesus was sleeping as usual in my little boat"[99] and was "going to no trouble about carrying on a conversation with me!"[100]

Thérèse's reaching for closeness to God increased after her arrival at Carmel, as she tried to assuage the pain of her beloved father's failing health and his mental decline. Thérèse's prayer intensified, but God continued to be silent. She tried to clasp onto Jesus for help, and Jesus didn't respond. When her father worsened and died, Thérèse was crushed. She had attempted to have her way with God, and she had failed.

Receiving God's Love Gratefully

Simple obedience was not an adequate way to love God. Thérèse also saw that it was impossible for her to compel a sense of intimacy with God by the sheer force of her desire. In her tears, the disconsolate Thérèse came to understand that God could not be seduced by her willfulness. She needed to purify her motives.

Thérèse still trusted that love was the answer. She continued to search for what love of God really looked like. Up against the limits of her efforts, she abandoned herself more fully into God's care for her. She had been longing for the emotional experience of closeness; now she stopped chasing that dream in a self-centered, ambitious way.

In her deep grief at the loss of her father, in her desolation and emptiness, a transformation was happening. As Thérèse surrendered her striving, a glimmering new awareness grew in her: the sense that God was in the pain, loving her in her weakness. She did not need to grasp for God, who was already present and had been present all along.

The vision opened before her as the dawning of a new day. Thérèse knew that she was not alone in her agony and that her father had not been alone in his agony. Seeing once more that her ways were not God's ways, Thérèse recognized that God was already holding her, her father, and everyone. God was acting in her life in ways she had not imagined before. God had been embracing her all this time, while she had been preoccupied with grasping God.

In the depths of her abandonment to the reality of God's present love, Thérèse entered a new phase in her spiritual growth. In this third phase, Thérèse focused on receiving gratefully what God was doing in her life and not on what she wanted God to do, nor on what she did for God. Thérèse grew from trying to please God through obedience, then trying to grasp God, to finally allowing God's way to prevail within her. She needed to love God on God's terms, and those terms were that God love her first. God didn't simply want obedience or to be desired in intimacy but to be fully welcomed by her.

Thérèse had an inkling of this truth when she experienced God's love in her conversion, as her contribution to that event was simply her goodwill. She began to live according to an image planted in her at that time: God desired to be received by her and by the whole human family. Thérèse's love was not to be the love of grasping but the love of fulfilling God's own *"thirst,"*[101] by receiving willingly and gratefully God's love. She recognized more fully that God did not need to be sought; God had already embraced her.

In the months and years after the loss of her father, Thérèse continued to love God in obedience, in charity, and in always seeking deeper intimacy in prayer. These aspects of her love continued, now empty of the willful spiritual ambition of youth. She could lay aside her early desire to love God more than anyone had ever loved before. Resting in God's arms and receiving that love—the foundation of her Little Way—now carried her forward.

This understanding of God's love is a profound and theologically sound insight, original to Thérèse's personal experiences. She grew into this awareness of God's loving presence from her prayerful reflections on the Gospels and the events of her own life, with little significant help from a spiritual director or books. She received it as gift.

Receiving God's Love with Gratitude

Thérèse's new consciousness of the love of God was personally transforming. It was a transformation largely unnoticed by others, though her companions in the convent noted a gradual relaxation in Thérèse's relationships with them.

The simple truth was that Thérèse's new posture of receiving God's love in gratitude allowed her to love herself and others more deeply, for she was loving with God's own love. Having previously said, "But creatures! ... those who surround me are very good, but there is something, I don't know what, that repels me! ... I cannot give you any explanation,"[102] Thérèse now recognized a deep truth: "[N]ever would I be able to love my Sisters as You love them, unless *You*, O My Jesus, *loved them in me*."[103]

Gratitude filled Thérèse's heart as she reflected on the truth of her life and the unmerited, ever-present love of God. Even though she faced problems and distress at times, she could quote the psalmist: "To me the Lord has always been 'merciful and good, slow to anger and abounding in steadfast love' (Psalm 102:8)," and, "Even though I walk through the valley of the shadow of death, I fear no evil; for you are with me" [Psalm 22].[104] Thérèse's gratitude released in her a healing and life-giving energy.

Thérèse went on to discover the essential calling that lies at the core of all vocations. She saw that without the primary motivation of love, *every* vocation becomes a selfish and eventually violent endeavor. She wrote with great joy, "O Jesus, my Love, . . . my vocation, at last I have found it, . . . MY VOCATION IS LOVE!"[105] Thérèse was seized with the power of this vision to *be* love at the heart of the Church, welcoming God's love on behalf of all the members of the Church, saints and sinners.

The discovery of her core vocation filled Thérèse with joy. It was the same joy she had when she realized that the spiritual life had an elevator, the lift of God's loving arms. In welcoming God's love and being completely available to God, Thérèse saw more clearly that her weakness and littleness were not obstacles. She need not be anything more than who she truly was.

The peace and joy that filled Thérèse confirmed the budding realization that it was not grandiose of her to be willing to be love at the heart of the Church. She would not, out of false humility, deny all the good things that God had given to her. She knew herself to be imperfect and yet also dearly beloved of God.

Thérèse returned again and again to these two core elements of the only treasure of the Little Way: recognizing her littleness and putting herself in God's arms. With both gratitude and joy, she wrote, "I must bear with myself such as I am with all my imperfections."[106] She saw that she was carried just this way by the God who loved her.

Thérèse shared her insight into the heart quality of gratefulness with those she mentored. With confidence she wrote, "Jesus does not demand great actions from us but simply *surrender* and *gratitude*."[107] Thérèse surrendered without fear or shame to the reality of who she was, grateful for God's unfailing love, willing to be imperfect because Jesus came for the imperfect.

This is the message that Thérèse recognized in the Gospel story (Luke 18:9-14) that contrasted the prayer of the wealthy, religiously observant Pharisee with the prayer of the publican, who was tainted by his dealings in the morally complex real world. The Pharisee's prayer consisted of telling God that he had been perfectly obedient, that he was as connected to God as he needed to be, and that all his moral accounts were in order. The publican stayed in the back of the Temple and kept his eyes lowered, acknowledging his sinfulness but welcoming God's love as he prayed, "O God, be merciful to me a sinner" (18:13).

Like the publican, Thérèse wanted to continually embrace God's mercy, even and especially in her sinfulness. At the end of her life, she made reference in her writings to how she wanted to go to God: "Rather than advance like the Pharisee, I repeat, filled with confidence, the publican's humble prayer."[108]

She would go to God by way of her imperfections. She was confident to the end in what she called her only treasure: the embrace of her littleness and her trust in God's merciful love.

The "Sacrament of the Present Moment"

Thérèse's insight into the loving providence of God grew wide and deep. She saw that this love was present to her always, in all circumstances. In her spirit of gratefulness, Thérèse surrendered herself to the actual joys and trials of her life, coming equally from God's providence.

The sisters in the convent experienced the maturing Thérèse as a person who was ordinarily calm and pleasant, a tranquil person. And yet she revealed in the honesty of her writings how often her days contained many painful emotional trials. Thérèse's mature understanding of God's love provides a key to her steady equanimity in the ups and downs of life. Embracing all her experiences as manifestations of God's presence and love, Thérèse understood that the present moment was filled with God's providence and love.

Thérèse began to receive the present moment as she would receive a sacrament. She received her life as it came to her, with trust that God's love was present always, regardless of the circumstances.

He nourishes me at each moment with a totally new food;
I find it within me without my knowing how it is there. . . .
He is giving me the grace of acting within me, making me
think of all He desires me to do at the present moment.[109]

This awareness enabled Thérèse to tap the creativity of love. In a spirit of gratefulness and trust, she surrendered herself in the moment and the situation, cooperating with God's love acting in and through her.

Mentoring Messages for Reflection

Ultimately, we recognize, as Thérèse did, that we don't need to search for love. God, the mystery and source of all love, is already within our hearts; we only need to welcome God's gift of love. Gratitude flows freely as we recognize this gift, even on our dark days.

Inspiring though this may be, the capacity to accept life in a grateful spirit may come slowly. In Thérèse's own story, we see that this all-encompassing gratefulness developed gradually. It was intimately connected to her growing insights into the mystery of God's love.

There are two mentoring messages suggested by Thérèse's countercultural spirit of gratefulness for everything that life brought to her. One has to do with how we think about life's sufferings; the other has to do with freedom from the trap of romantic ideals about a perfect life, partner, or job.

✧ A grateful spirit doesn't erase all pain and suffering from our lives; if we love, we will experience both joy and sorrow.

In mentoring us, Thérèse might observe how we are influenced by our early ways of understanding and relating to

God. These ideas condition our ability to feel gratitude. For example, perhaps we were raised with the belief that God is constantly making specific decisions about whether to reward or punish us. If so, it makes sense that we might feel resentful about the life experiences that are trouble for us.

But Thérèse didn't see God acting that way. Thérèse came to know and trust a loving God who accompanies us as our life unfolds in the complex created world. She didn't see God making moment-by-moment judgments on our worthiness and sending us consequences to match.

Thérèse's grateful welcoming of God's love, in every experience of her life, offers us a liberating viewpoint. We know there will be pain, and there will be joy, and we don't have to be afraid. We can face what is real and live through it, with confidence that in the big picture, all will be well.

A skeptical voice within us might say, "Perhaps." When we're faced with tough times, the part of us that is reality-weary may be tempted to wave off this vision as sentimental and naïve. We think, Isn't it obvious that all kinds of sorrow will touch our lives? Is that supposed to be good? What if we feel angry at God for the things that bring us sorrow and pain?

Thérèse was not blind to the truth of a painfully flawed world. She was deeply saddened by the illness and death of her beloved father. But Thérèse didn't see life's losses as punishments by an unsympathetic, cruel God, deliberately inflicting pain on her. Thérèse understood human pain as an inevitable part of a loving human life.

At some level, we also know that truth. We learn from the school of life that the same love that is a source of joy can also bring us grief. We might lose a dear one or feel betrayed by someone we love or suffer the loss of activities we once treasured. Feelings remain feelings, and just as we feel heat in the presence of fire, so we will feel pain and sorrow in our losses.

It was her grateful willingness to trust in God's love that eventually brought Thérèse joy and peace. And we see from her life that there is no fast and easy route to that spirit of trust and gratitude. She came to more than one dead end in her desire to love God. Her path led her through grief and loss. We are likely to have similar experiences.

The good thing about the heart quality of gratefulness is that we can cultivate this attitude through reflection. With practice we can come to see more of the beauty and blessing that come to us each day. With trust we can discover a way to bear difficult days with patient steadiness. Our gratitude is for life itself and for the mystery and power of love.

✧ A spirit of gratitude for our real life can free us to live faithfully in a world full of imperfect people, relationships, and circumstances.

By her grateful welcome of God's providence in all moments, Thérèse shows how to stop chasing illusory visions of a perfect life. Despite her rapturous aspirations of becoming a priest, a martyr, or a crusader, Thérèse was no romantic dreamer. She lived with joy and daily fidelity her calling as a Carmelite sister in the small and ordinary convent at Lisieux. She models how to live faithfully with our real and imperfect relationships, trusting that God's love will animate our hearts and our actions and keep us on the path of love.

God's love for us is real and always present. This means that there is no point in sitting paralyzed and burdened, waiting for greener pastures: that imagined time when we have the perfect mate or job, when we will be thin or wealthy or successful, when we will have everything in our home organized and under control, when the nation and the world are not in a crisis of some kind. Such dreams are illusions. They mask the reality that our life happens in the present moment. We are called to receive and share God's love as it is available to us in each moment—in *this* present moment.

This awareness is empowering and energizing, filling us with gratitude for the gift of our lives. If God's love for us and the world is present to us *here* and *now* and *always*, through both joy and sorrow, then there is a way for us to be at peace. We can live a more relaxed life, coming alive creatively and compassionately in inner freedom, here and now.

Anyone who has worked up the courage to commit to marriage, parenthood, or a lifetime vow has come face-to-face with the same huge heart risk: the promise to give one's love and one's life now and every day, in the midst of whatever real life presents to us. There is no need to wait; we fulfill our vocation to be love at the heart of God's family when we move through our ordinary real life with an attitude of grateful love.

We don't need to wait for a better time to make a difference in the world, to act justly, to love our enemy, or to speak up for those with no voice. This is true even when we need to make corrective changes in our lives in order to live with greater integrity. It is true even when we need to set boundaries to help us bear in love what we cannot change for the better.

The stance of gratitude for the always present love of God, the sacrament of the present moment, is a counterweight to quests of all kinds, including seductions of the prosperity gospel that may tempt us from the self-help bookshelf. The prosperity gospel is a modern version of an old misconception about God. It implies that if we hold fast to the "right" beliefs and work hard at our goals, the Higher Power will reward us with material success and happiness. The cruel implication is that those who suffer or fail are responsible for their own troubles.

The logic of the prosperity gospel denies what Thérèse grew to understand: the gift and mystery of life in our complex world unfolds within us each day, and the immensity of Love that we call God doesn't love us any more if we enjoy abundance, nor any less if we bear with hardship. A grateful spirit arises within us when our hearts register the joy, relief, and confidence of knowing ourselves to be loved and loveable. If there is a song that comes with the heart qualities of Thérèse's Little Way, it is the song of gratitude.

Chapter 12

Love Is Self-Surrender

Is surrender a good thing or a bad thing? In the wider culture, surrender is usually the equivalent of defeat. It means we have met a force we cannot overcome and to which we must yield. As defeat, surrender brings with it feelings of shame and failure. It leaves us feeling flattened, empty, powerless.

And yet poets also speak of the times we surrender ourselves to a true love or to the experience of awesome beauty in nature, art, music, or dance. That implies that we have set aside barriers that block our hearts and have opened ourselves vulnerably to the power of the moment. We are filled, moved, empowered.

In either case—defeated or transformed—the dynamic of surrender goes beyond the limits of what our egos can control. That's a notion that can make us feel afraid and anxious, especially when we face problems. In such circumstances, we valiantly do our best.

Is there any value for us in the idea of self-surrender? What is life-giving about self-surrender? What does it even mean?

Self-Surrender as Total Trust

Self-surrender, as Thérèse understood it, was her trusting response to God, knowing that she was safe, cared for, and cherished by God in every moment. Self-surrender expressed and at the same time nurtured Thérèse's inner freedom, as well as the other heart qualities of her Little Way. This surrender supported her compassion and creativity, and it fostered willingness and gratefulness in her.

For Thérèse, self-surrender had nothing of the cultural under-current of giving up or of defeat. To begin with, she wasn't at war against any of her experiences, even the most difficult ones. Thérèse used the term "self-surrender" to describe how she lived with a loving energy, free from the need to have things go her way. Self-surrender liberated her from the weight of being in control and the urge to bully.

Even in difficult times, Thérèse clung to her confidence in God's love, just as she saw Jesus trusting fully in his Father. Jesus prayed in anguish in the Garden of Gethsemane on the night before he was executed. Yet from within his agonized heart, he freely surrendered himself to God, whom he trusted with his life and with his death: "Father, if you are willing, take this cup away from me; still, not my will but yours be done" (Luke 22:42).

For Thérèse, as for Jesus, the attitude of self-surrender reached an apex as her own death drew near. Although she had thought of herself as prepared to suffer illness and let go of her life whenever God would call her, Thérèse did not expect the anguishing spiritual and psychological trial of her final illness. In this chapter, we witness the courage with which Thérèse endured those final days, her sense of solidarity with atheists, her temptations to suicide, and her enduring trust and love even in the face of darkness. She teaches us that maturity, meaning, joy, and peace come when we welcome God's love without fear or bitterness.

Death Announces Its Approach

Thérèse realized she was ill when she coughed up blood on Good Friday in the spring of 1896. At first the unmistakable signal of her failing health filled Thérèse with joyful fervor: *"It was like a sweet and distant murmur that announced the Bridegroom's arrival."* She rejoiced that Jesus had given her the "sign that my entrance into eternal life was not far off."[110]

Thérèse must have felt the instinctive physical urge that everyone feels to keep living and not die, but she was accustomed to "enjoying such a living faith, such a clear faith" that she didn't harbor a fear of death.[111] She had always looked forward to a heaven in which she would be completely embraced by God's life and love and be reunited with her father, her mother, and the siblings who had died in infancy. She anticipated seeing Mary, the mother of Jesus, and being with the angels and saints. And she yearned to do good on earth after her death.

But Thérèse unexpectedly plunged into a dreadful personal darkness that blocked her deepest longings. The pervading aridity and spiritual desolation deeply frightened her at times. It was a devastating turn.

[Jesus] permitted my soul to be invaded by the thickest darkness, and that the thought of heaven, up until then so sweet to me, be no longer anything but the cause of struggle and torment. . . . One would have to travel through this dark tunnel to understand its darkness.[112]

With somber honesty, she wrote to her superior, "My dear Mother, I may perhaps appear to you to be exaggerating my trial. . . . I must appear to you as a soul filled with consolations." But now, unable to anticipate the joys of heaven, Thérèse faced "a wall which reaches right up to the heavens and covers the starry firmament. When I sing of the happiness of heaven and of the eternal possession of God, I feel no joy in this, for I sing simply what I WANT TO BELIEVE."[113]

Unexpectedly, Thérèse experienced the doubt of the atheist and the agnostic. She wondered if there was really a heaven or if her hope in God was a foolish fable.

Into the Darkness

By her own account, earlier in her life, Thérèse simply couldn't imagine atheism. "I was unable to believe there were really impious people who had no faith."[114] Sadly, a distressing event during Thérèse's illness brought home to her the fact that, yes, some people didn't believe in God, and some also had the evil intention of darkening the faith of others.

In those days, the front pages of newspapers in France tracked the captivating story of the French writer Léo Taxil and his companion, Diana Vaughan, who had announced their conversions from Freemasonry and Satanism to Catholicism. This dramatic news spread even to the Carmel of Lisieux, and it fascinated the sisters, inspiring them to send a supportive note to Diana. Because Diana was said to have a special devotion to St. Joan of Arc, Pauline included with the note a photo of Thérèse dressed as Joan of Arc, from her performance in a play she'd written for the convent.

A short time later, under pressure for a personal interview, Léo Taxil called a national press conference to introduce Diana, who had been in hiding for months in various convents. To the shock of the several hundred news reporters present, Taxil announced that the whole story had been a hoax. He had never converted to Catholicism. Further, he had drafted Diana Vaughn, a secretary in his employ, as an accomplice in his efforts to discredit the Church. Mocking the naïve faith of Catholics in general and of Carmelite nuns in particular, he had projected on the screen behind him the photo of Thérèse dressed as Joan of Arc.

This mean-spirited trick was a deep and personal wound for Thérèse, a painful betrayal and public humiliation. She tore up a thank you note from Diana and threw it away. Holding to her Little Way, however, she surrendered her bruised dignity and prayed for the grace to love her enemies.

Thérèse prayed for compassion for those who, she now saw, really didn't believe in God. Furthermore, she recognized the common ground that she shared with them as she endured the "darkness I am plunged into." [115]

It seems to me that the darkness . . . says mockingly to me:
"You are dreaming about the light. . . . [Y]ou believe that
one day you will walk out of this fog that surrounds you! . . .
[R]ejoice in death which will give you not what you hope for
but a night still more profound, the night of nothingness."[116]

In this unexpected spiritual darkness, Thérèse honestly
named her fears and doubts. "I don't believe in eternal life; I
think that after this life there is nothing. Everything has dis-
appeared on me."[117]

Calling those without faith her brothers and sisters, Thérèse
prayed for them:

May all those who were not enlightened by the bright flame
of faith one day see it shine. . . . I desire to eat this bread of
trial at this table until it pleases You to bring me into Your
bright Kingdom. [118]

By her own account and the testimony of others, Thérèse
suffered terribly in the last months of her illness. Most medi-
cations were unavailable in the austerity of Carmelite life, and
so she experienced horrible physical pain as the tuberculosis
robbed her of breath. Her physical suffering compounded her
psychological and spiritual anguish. In the darkness of her torment, she even had thoughts of suicide.

To the sister caring for her, she said,

Watch carefully, Mother, when you will have patients a prey
to violent pains; don't leave near them any medicines that
are poisonous. I assure you, it needs only a second when one

suffers intensely to lose one's reason. Then one would easily poison oneself.[119]

Thérèse understood her vocation, to be love "in the heart of the Church."[120] Through her suffering, she now saw how wide that heart of love really was. It embraced the confused and the aimless, the atheist and the agnostic, the suicidal, and even herself at the edge of hope and faith. Stripped of all consolation, Thérèse could do nothing but surrender her desire to escape the fog. She simply embraced God's will at the moment of nothingness and emptiness and did what she could to cling to the path of love. "I am left with love alone."[121]

Love at Faith's Limits

Thérèse wrote and spoke of her doubts only sparingly, admitting her distress to the few companions who would not be scandalized or think her insane. She wrote, "I don't want to write any longer about it; I fear I might blaspheme; I fear even that I have already said too much."[122]

Consequently, Thérèse's inner trial was mostly invisible to others. To the sisters who came to visit her in the infirmary, Thérèse showed as much kindness and patience as she could muster in her weakened physical state. She was the same kind Thérèse they had known, tranquil and humorous. Her cousin, Sr. Marie of the Eucharist, wrote, "As far as her morale is concerned, it is always the same: cheerfulness itself. She is always making those who come to visit her laugh. There are times when one would pay to be near her."[123]

Thérèse wrote, "[E]xteriorly nothing revealed my suffering, which was all the more painful since I alone was aware of it."[124] Her attention to managing her emotions enabled her to remain patient with her inner distress. She could surrender herself to God's providence in the situation at hand. In fact, she wrote many beautiful poems and prayers during this time.

Her last eighteen months of life constituted a severe purification of Thérèse's soul, burning away traces of self-centeredness, vanity, and ambition. Her trial meant the abandonment of her self-image, even the abandonment of her aspiration to die "the right way," the way she and the other sisters thought a holy Carmelite sister should die. She humbly accepted the fact that her inability to swallow meant she could not receive Communion, normally a holy moment in the "right" way of dying. To console those accompanying her, she said, "Without a doubt, it's a great grace to receive the sacraments; but when God doesn't allow it, it's good just the same; everything is a grace."[125]

Aware of the anguish revealed in her account of her last months, Thérèse wrote, "[M]y little story which resembled a fairy tale is all of a sudden changed into a prayer."[126] It was a prayer, we might add, of desperation. This woman knew she was scraping the bottom of her personal and spiritual resources. In her honesty, Thérèse accepted the reality that she felt the blackness of doubt and that she had thoughts of suicide. There remained no idea about heaven or feeling of consolation to hold on to, other than her unfailing conviction that love is all that matters.

Thérèse continued to open her heart to the love of God and to hope in God's faithfulness.

The words of Job: "Even though he should kill me, yet will I trust him," always fascinated me in my childhood days. It took me a long time, however, to reach that degree of surrender. Now I have reached it; God has placed me in this degree, for He has taken me up into His arms and placed me there."[127]

Thérèse had surrendered her living to God; now she surrendered her dying to him—by being patient with herself and with her sisters and by receiving the sacrament of the present moment with gratefulness, without bitterness or resentment.

Earlier Thérèse had written a prayer, the Act of Oblation to Merciful Love, which includes:

In the evening of this life, I shall appear before You with empty hands, for I do not ask You, Lord, to count my works. All our justice is stained in Your eyes. I wish, then, to be clothed in Your own *Justice* and to receive from Your *Love* the eternal possession of *Yourself*.[128]

By surrendering her life to God, praying as Jesus had prayed in the Garden of Gethsemane, Thérèse joined her suffering to the redemptive death of Jesus. The love that carried her was like a consuming fire, dissolving images and feelings with which she had made sense of the mystery of God. She wrote, "[W]hile I do not have *the joy of faith*, I am trying to carry out its works at least. I believe I have made more acts of faith in this past year than all through my whole life."[129]

Thérèse's surrender was not just the poverty of accomplishments but the inner poverty of complete surrender into the arms of God. Her surrender was a courageous leap in the dark, carried by love alone. At the last, Thérèse still cherished what she called her only treasure:

> I understand so well that it is only love that makes us accept-
> able to God, that this love is the only good I ambition. . . .
> [T]his road is the *surrender* of the little child who sleeps
> without fear in its Father's arms.[130]

Now love overtook the doctrines, the theology, and the spiritual formulas that were failing Thérèse in her suffering. At the limit of her hope, willingly embracing even her emptiness, she clung to her confidence that God is love and love is real.

Thérèse refused to abandon her Little Way, even when it seemed an illusion. Her courage, strength of will, and passionate trust in God did not desert her. She continued in her long-held conviction that after death, she would do good on earth. She would fulfill her vocation, even in heaven, to be love at the heart of God's family.

Thérèse of Lisieux died on September 30, 1897, at the age of twenty-four, in peace and joy, with a final expression of love.

Mentoring Messages for Reflection

How are we to take life lessons from the last days of Thérèse's story? This final, agonizing period of her life is tough to witness. Ironically, this part of her story may be the one with which we can most identify. Here we see Thérèse as a normal person, like us. No one can sugarcoat her suffering.

Her lessons of self-surrender here are difficult to absorb but crucial.

✧ Love opens us to suffering that we cannot avoid and brings us to the threshold of self-surrender.

We can feel as if we're scraping bottom even if we aren't facing a terminal illness. There are many situations that we can't control and that can overwhelm us, especially if they affect those we love. Perhaps the deeper meaning of the heart quality of self-surrender is most apparent when we have no choice but to face a life event that we absolutely wish to avoid.

We may have to confront grave illness. Or tragic suffering may come from the violence of others, a child lost to alcoholism or drugs, incarceration, incapacitation through a freak accident, loss of a job, natural disaster, war, or worldwide disease. Up to a point, we can take on such problems as things to deal with somehow. But eventually we are brought to our knees—empty, devastated, frustrated, or angry. We may be at the threshold of surrender to the larger providence of God.

Self-surrender is not victimhood; neither is it victory. Self-surrender is an embrace of reality as we encounter it in the created world. It is acknowledging that we don't control reality, which inevitably consists of both suffering and joy.

Suffering is what Thérèse often referred to as the "fire" that purifies the heart. This is not because God is punishing us but because life will bring us sorrow if it is lived with love. We can hope for the grace to do our best: to remain loving in truly difficult circumstances, compassionate both to ourselves and to others, holding on to the truth no matter what. Thérèse teaches us to trust in the ultimate power of Love, despite the impossibility of seeing through the dark.

✧ Willingness to let go of our own needs and comfort zones is the daily attitude of self-surrender, which helps us toward a loving life.

Even in the ordinary, undramatic realities of daily life, there is a place for the heart quality of self-surrender. It's a subtle quality that pervades each of Thérèse's vignettes of convent life. Thérèse, our mentor, shows us how a capacity for self-surrender can mark our increasing spiritual and psychological maturity.

There will be moments when our ego wants to argue for a different path than the loving way. Acting with compassion and kindness can be costly to our comfort, pride, and preferences. We sometimes have to get quite far out of our comfort zone if we want to meet the needs of another person on *their* terms, not ours. Like Thérèse, we can seek a loving energy that is free of the need to have things our way. Often these times of self-surrender will be hidden from outside view. They are likely to happen during our times of honest self-reflection.

We surrender the need to be at the center of our own life dramas, as we tame excessive emotional reactions and learn not to take our feelings personally.

We surrender our defensiveness and competitiveness, learning to hold our tongue and avoiding the temptation to hurt another and come out on top.

We surrender our wish to injure our enemies, and we seek to look with compassion on wounded hearts—our own heart and the hearts of those who cause us pain.

We surrender our need for control, as we learn to accept with gratitude the gift that life offers us at every moment—both the pleasing and the difficult experiences—and to respond to those moments creatively.

We even surrender our belief in our own strength, when we feel pushed beyond our limits. Surrendering the false image of power, we can embrace our human reality and maintain our hope in the power of love.

✧ Self-surrender is a paradox, a heart action that we can take even when we are most vulnerable.

Self-surrender is the free act of welcoming God's loving presence and care for us in the reality of the present moment. In the act of self-surrender, we experience release from our own inner need for control, for potency. Self-surrender is a paradox: a heart action that moves us away from a sense of danger and opens us to trust and hope.

It may be hard to wrap our minds around this. At the very time when we are out of options, at our limit, unable to cope— like the little boy having a meltdown at the theme park—we have at least one option left: to let go of the struggle and embrace the truth. As the quiet presence of the staffer comforted that little boy, we can let the tension drain away as we acknowledge that we are not abandoned. Love endures.

Thérèse's guidance is simple, yet it has power to bring healing and peace to troubled hearts. The example of Thérèse and that of Jesus gently encourage us to surrender our agonized hearts to the God who is all love. During her personal trial of faith and her embrace of love, Thérèse showed us how an ordinary person can bear with the suffering that life brings. In surrendering ourselves to God's providence in the present moment, we too can hope for the grace to hold fast, confident that Love has the last word.

Conclusion

O ur search for a meaningful, peaceful, joyful life doesn't have to be a solitary quest. *We have what we need.* Acknowledging our ever-present weakness, we can dare to claim Thérèse's only treasure. That treasure was her confidence that her imperfections did not stop God from loving her at every moment. God's love flowing through her heart was the source of Thérèse's joyful and kind spirit.

Like Thérèse, we can grow in grace and love by cultivating the heart qualities that signal we are on the right path: inner freedom, compassion, creativity, a willing spirit, gratefulness, and self-surrender. As we welcome the fact that we are unfailingly loved in every moment, we open ourselves to the grace of being changed and healed.

It may seem that the mentoring messages inspired by Thérèse in this book are focused on small things. Are they up to the ongoing challenges we encounter in our relationships, our society, and our workplaces? We hope you will find that the answer is yes. When our own hearts change, the world changes, even if just a little bit.

The wisdom Thérèse offers us operates quietly on the *inside* of our active life in the world. She doesn't tell us which commitments to choose or which career to pursue, but she guides the spirit with which we might go about our work, our studies, and our relationships. One small step at a time, she shows us the way to emotional and spiritual maturity.

We will never be perfect; with relief we recognize that being perfect isn't necessary for a loving, meaningful life. We have gifts, and we have flaws, but we will never be beyond the reach of the Great Love. As we take our small steps on the way of love, like Thérèse, our mentor, we may begin to notice our days becoming less combative and more relaxed, more joyful and more fruitful. Thérèse's way and example will help us live our unique life authentically, free to bring our personal gifts to our corner of the world.

Indeed, why would this treasure not be ours?

Acknowledgements

This book came together with the unflagging support of many dear friends and colleagues. We are grateful for their insights and for the encouragement they provided to keep us on the writing journey. Whenever we asked, they graciously agreed to read early drafts and patiently provided invaluable feedback.

For their many and varied generous contributions, we are thankful to: John Traveline, MD; Gilbert D'Alonzo, DO; Msgr. Francis X. Schmidt; Kate Ward-Gaus; Maureen Tate; Timothy Fallon; Karol Wasylyshyn, PhD; Al and Betsy Puntel; Kate Dempsey, PhD; Ken E. Houston; Sr. Patty Fawkner, SGS; Michael J. Guerin; Sr. Vicki Schwartz, SL; Sr. Mary Trainer, RSM; Sr. Maria DiBello, RSM; Sr. Rose Anthony, ASC; James Johnson; Mary DiVito; Clinton Williams; Msgr. Richard Malone, Helen McBride; Sr. Carol Barnes, SC; Angela Coghlan; Brother Bernard LoCoco, FSC; and Mike Sweeney. Please forgive any omissions, and know that we are grateful to the many friends who regularly checked in with us as this project was unfolding.

We are also deeply indebted to the skillful editors and publisher at The Word Among Us Press. With patience, diplomacy, keen eyes, and understanding hearts, they helped us to make this a better book. Sincerest of thanks for their faith in this book.

Notes

A Note for Readers

1. Thérèse of Lisieux, *Story of a Soul: The Autobiography of Saint Thérèse of Lisieux*, trans. John Clarke, 3rd ed. (Washington, D.C.: Institute of Carmelite Studies, 1996), 158.

Chapter 1: Thérèse and Her "Only Treasure"

2. *Story of a Soul*,15.
3. *Story of a Soul*,13.
4. *Story of a Soul*, 23.
5. *Story of a Soul*, 22.
6. *Story of a Soul*, 101.
7. *Story of a Soul*, 91.
8. Thérèse of Lisieux, *General Correspondence: Letters of St. Thérèse of Lisieux*, vol. 2, trans. John Clarke, OCD (Washington, D.C.: Institute of Carmelite Studies, 1988), 778.
9. Pope John Paul II, *Divini Amoris Scientia* [Apostolic Letter, St. Thérèse of the Child Jesus and the Holy Face Is Proclaimed a Doctor of the Universal Church], October 19, 1997, 8, vatican.va/content/john-paul-ii/en/apost_letters/1997/documents/hf_jp-ii_apl_19101997_divini-amoris.html.
10. *General Correspondence*, vol. 2, 999.
11. *General Correspondence*, vol. 2, 999.

Chapter 2: Freeing the Captives

12. *Story of a Soul*, 34-35.
13. *Story of a Soul*, 97.
14. *Story of a Soul*, 34.
15. *Story of a Soul*, 58.
16. *Story of a Soul*, 58.
17. *Story of a Soul*, 88.
18. *Story of a Soul*, 97.
19. *Story of a Soul*, 98.
20. *Story of a Soul*, 97.
21. *Story of a Soul*, 98.

Chapter 3: Resurrecting the God of Love

22. Pope John Paul II, 8.
23. *Story of a Soul*, 180.
24. Pierre Descouvemont, *Thérèse of Lisieux and Marie of the Trinity* (New York: Alba House, 1997), 75.
25. *Story of a Soul*, 99.
26. Descouvemont, 77.
27. Martin Luther King, Jr., *Strength to Love* (New York: Harper and Row, 1963), 47.

Chapter 4: What Is Love? And Learning What Love Is Not

28. *Story of a Soul*, 223.
29. Thomas Merton, *Conjectures of a Guilty Bystander* (Garden City, NY: Doubleday, 1966), 81.

Chapter 5: Healing from Perfectionism

30. *Story of a Soul*, 97.
31. *Story of a Soul*, 174.
32. *Story of a Soul*, 207.
33. *Story of a Soul*, 208.
34. *Story of a Soul*, 207.
35. *Story of a Soul*, 224.
36. *Story of a Soul*, 14.
37. *General Correspondence*, vol. 2, 1092.
38. *Story of a Soul*, 158.
39. *General Correspondence*, vol. 2, 1122.
40. Sr. Geneviève of the Holy Face, *My Sister St. Thérèse* (Rockford, IL: Tan Books, 1997), 28.
41. Sr. Geneviève, 28.
42. F. J. Sheed, trans., *Collected Letters of Saint Thérèse of Lisieux* (New York: Sheed and Ward, 1949), 303.
43. Thérèse of Lisieux, *St. Thérèse of Lisieux: Her Last Conversations*, John Clarke, OCD, trans. (Washington, D.C.: Institute of Carmelite Studies. 1977), 129, note 1.

Chapter 6: A Life Worth Living

44. *Story of a Soul*, 71.
45. *Story of a Soul*, 37.
46. *Story of a Soul*, 74–75.
47. *Story of a Soul*, 74.
48. *Story of a Soul*, 179.
49. *Story of a Soul*, 242.

50. *Story of a Soul*, 165.

51. *Story of a Soul*, 270, Epilogue.

52. *General Correspondence*, vol. 2, 1164.

53. *General Correspondence*, vol. 2, 1153.

Chapter 7: Love Is Inner Freedom

54. *Story of a Soul*, 39.

55. *Story of a Soul*, 250.

56. *Story of a Soul*, 237.

57. *Story of a Soul*, 224.

58. *Story of a Soul*, 158.

59. *Story of a Soul*, 91.

60. *Story of a Soul*, 261 Epilogue.

Chapter 8: Love Is Compassion

61. *Story of a Soul*, 225.

62. *Story of a Soul*, 226.

63. *Story of a Soul*, 257.

64. *Story of a Soul*, 222.

65. *Story of a Soul*, 223.

66. *Story of a Soul*, 248.

67. *Story of a Soul*, 246.

68. Christopher O'Mahony, trans. and ed., *St. Thérèse of Lisieux by Those Who Knew Her* (Huntington, IN: Our Sunday Visitor, 1975), 50–51.

69. *Story of a Soul*, 224.

70. *Her Last Conversations*, 38.

71. *Story of a Soul*, 223

Chapter 9: Love Is Creativity

72. *Story of a Soul*, 89.

73. *Story of a Soul*, 89.

74. *Story of a Soul*, 101.

75. *Story of a Soul*, 140.

76. *Story of a Soul*,134–135.

77. *Story of a Soul*, 249.

78. *Story of a Soul*, 250.

79. O'Mahony, 31.

80. Sr. Geneviève, 118.

81. *Story of a Soul*, 192.

82. *Story of a Soul*, 223.

Chapter 10: Love Is a Willing Spirit

83. *Story of a Soul*, 39.

84. *Story of a Soul*, 27.

85. *Story of a Soul*, 98.

86. *Story of a Soul*, 143.

87. *Story of a Soul*, 143.

88. *Story of a Soul*, 238.

89. Descouvemont, 114.

90. T. S. Eliot, *Murder in the Cathedral* (New York, NY: Harcourt, Inc., 1963), 44.

Chapter 11: Love Is Gratefulness

91. *Story of a Soul*, 188.
92. *Story of a Soul*, 38.
93. *Story of a Soul*, 194.
94. *Story of a Soul*, 29.
95. *Story of a Soul*, 97.
96. *General Correspondence*, vol. 1, 500.
97. *General Correspondence*, vol. 1, 500.
98. *General Correspondence*, vol. 1, 500.
99. *Story of a Soul*, 165.
100. *General Correspondence*, vol. 1, 500.
101. *Story of a Soul*, 99.
102. *General Correspondence*, vol. 1, 500,
103. *Story of a Soul*, 221.
104. *Story of a Soul*, 15.
105. *Story of a Soul*, 194.
106. *Story of a Soul*, 207.
107. *Story of a Soul*, 188.
108. *Story of a Soul*, 258.
109. *Story of a Soul*, 165.

Chapter 12: Love Is Self-Surrender

110. *Story of a Soul*, 211.
111. *Story of a Soul*, 211.
112. *Story of a Soul*, 211–212.
113. *Story of a Soul*, 214.
114. *Story of a Soul*, 211.

115. O'Mahony, 195.
116. *Story of a Soul*, 213.
117. O'Mahony, 195.
118. *Story of a Soul*, 212..
119. *Her Last Conversations*, 258.
120. *Story of a Soul*, 194.
121. O'Mahony, 195.
122. *Story of a Soul*, 213.
123. *Story of a Soul*, Epilogue, 265.
124. *Story of a Soul*, 149.
125. *Her Last Conversations*, 57.
126. *Story of a Soul*, 212;
127. *Story of a Soul*, 267, Epilogue.
128. *Story of a Soul*, 277.
129. *Story of a Soul*, 213.
130. *Story of a Soul*, 188.

References

Descouvemont, Pierre. *Thérèse of Lisieux and Marie of the Trinity*. New York: Alba House, 1997.

Sr. Geneviève of the Holy Face (Céline Martin). *My Sister St. Thérèse*. Rockford, IL: Tan Books, 1997.

O'Mahony, Christopher, trans. and ed. *St. Thérèse of Lisieux by Those Who Knew Her*. Huntington, IN: Our Sunday Visitor, 1975.

Pope John Paul II. *Divini Amoris Scientia* [Apostolic Letter, St. Thérèse of the Child Jesus and the Holy Face Is Proclaimed a Doctor of the Universal Church]. October 19, 1997. vatican.va/content/john-paul-ii/en/apost_letters/1997/documents/hf_jp-ii_apl_19101997_divini-amoris.html.

Sheed, F. J., trans. *Collected Letters of Saint Thérèse of Lisieux*. New York: Sheed and Ward, 1949.

Thérèse of Lisieux. *General Correspondence: Letters of St. Thérèse of Lisieux*. Translated by John Clarke, OCD. 2 vols. Washington, DC: Institute of Carmelite Studies, 1988.

Thérèse of Lisieux. *St. Thérèse of Lisieux: Her Last Conversations*. Translated by John Clarke, O.C.D. Washington, DC: Institute of Carmelite Studies, 1977.

Thérèse of Lisieux, *The Story of a Soul: The Autobiography of Saint Thérèse of Lisieux*. Translated by John Clarke, OCD. 3rd ed. Washington, D.C.: Institute of Carmelite Studies, 1996.

About the Authors

Joseph F. Schmidt, FSC, was a beloved author, lecturer, spiritual director, and retreat leader. He was the author of the highly acclaimed and bestselling *Everything Is Grace: The Life and Way of Thérèse of Lisieux*, as well as *Praying with Thérèse of Lisieux* and *Praying Our Experiences*.

Marisa Guerin, PhD, is a writer, retreat leader, and expert in organizational effectiveness and leadership development. During her career, she led the youth ministry office of the US Catholic Bishops, served as the senior Human Resources executive of a global company, and managed her own business as a consultant to religious institutes in the US and abroad. Now retired, Marisa is married to Michael B. Sweeney and lives in Philadelphia, Pennsylvania. Her articles and professional papers are available at www.guerinconsulting.com.

Dedication

*L*ife Lessons from St. Thérèse of Lisieux is dedicated to the memory of Br. Joseph Schmidt, FSC. Br. Joseph was a beloved author, retreat leader, educator, spiritual director, and a life-long friend of St. Thérèse of Lisieux. He passed away on February 19, 2022, shortly after this shared writing project was completed. Br. Joseph was respected internationally as a foremost scholar of the teachings of Thérèse. Through his many books, Br. Joseph brought the person and wisdom of Thérèse to life for thousands of contemporary readers. He is remembered with affection and gratitude by all those whose lives he touched.

Other Books by
Joseph Schmidt, FSC

Praying with Thérèse of Lisieux

This book seeks to engage the reader in praying in the way St. Thérèse did about issues and themes that were central to her experience. It contains reflections, meditations, and invitations to various forms of prayer.

Everything Is Grace: The Life and Way of Thérèse of Lisieux

This comprehensive biography of St. Thérèse offers insight into the psychological and spiritual journey of this saint. It weaves her autobiography, poems, and letters together with the perspective of our times. Reviewers highlight the fact that this book engages both the mind and the heart, helping this great saint step off its pages into the twenty-first century.

Walking the Little Way of Thérèse of Lisieux: Discovering the Path of Love

Thérèse struggled as we all do with emotional scars from her early years, and she grew in wisdom through her gift of prayerful reflection. This book opens for us the spiritual and psychological development of Thérèse over her lifetime.

The Gospel According to St. Thérèse: A Faith-Sharing Guide

Br. Joseph Schmidt helps readers understand Thérèse's message through the Scripture passages that illuminated her insights about God and his merciful love. Each of the seven sessions features one or more passages from Scripture as well as excerpts from Thérèse's writings that allude to those passages. Thoughtful commentary and questions for reflection follow, enabling us to discover how our own relationship with God might be transformed by the Little Way of St. Thérèse. Especially suitable for use by small groups.

the WORD among us®

The *Spirit* of Catholic Living

This book was published by The Word Among Us. Since 1981, The Word Among Us has been answering the call of the Second Vatican Council to help Catholic laypeople encounter Christ in the Scriptures.

The name of our company comes from the prologue to the Gospel of John and reflects the vision and purpose of all of our publications: to be an instrument of the Spirit, whose desire is to manifest Jesus' presence in and to the children of God. In this way, we hope to contribute to the Church's ongoing mission of proclaiming the gospel to the world so that all people would know the love and mercy of our Lord and grow more deeply in their faith as missionary disciples.

Our monthly devotional magazine, *The Word Among Us*, features meditations on the daily and Sunday Mass readings, and currently reaches more than one million Catholics in North America and another half million Catholics in one hundred countries around the world. Our book division, The Word Among Us Press, publishes numerous books, Bible studies, and pamphlets that help Catholics grow in their faith.

To learn more about who we are and what we publish, log on to our website at www.wau.org. There you will find a variety of Catholic resources that will help you grow in your faith.

Embrace His Word, Listen to God . . .

Made in United States
Orlando, FL
31 July 2023

35622092R00114